The
Pocket Guide
to
Poets and Poetry

The Pocket Guide to Poets and Poetry

Andrew Taylor

First published in Great Britain in 2011 by
REMEMBER WHEN
an imprint of
Pen & Sword Books Ltd
47 Church Street
Barnsley
South Yorkshire
S70 2AS

ISBN 978-1-84468-088-7

A CIP cataloge record for this book is available from the British Library

Typeset by Concept, West Yorkshire
Printed and bound in England by CPI UK

Pen & Sword Books Ltd incorporates the Imprints of Pen & Sword
Aviation, Pen & Sword Maritime, Pen & Sword Military, Wharncliffe
Local History, Pen & Sword Select, Pen & Sword Military Classics,
Leo Cooper, Remember When, Seaforth Publishing and Frontline
Publishing.

For a complete list of Pen & Sword titles please contact
PEN & SWORD BOOKS LIMITED
47 Church Street, Barnsley, South Yorkshire, S70 2AS, England
E-mail: enquiries@pen-and-sword.co.uk
Website: www.pen-and-sword.co.uk

Contents

Contents

The Pocket Guide to Poets and Poetry

Contents

Contents

Acknowledgements

THERE ARE a number of people I need to thank for their help in preparing this book – not least the staffs of the Oxford's Bodleian Library, the British Library, and the London Library, who have all been unfailingly patient as I pestered them for books and references.

Pat Roberts of www.blackandwhitephotos.biz, Richard Bretton, and Peter Murphy have generously lent me their talents as photographers. Individual photographs are acknowledged in the text. The books which are shown came from the extensive collection of Henry Sotheran's Fine Books and Prints, of Piccadilly, London, and I am grateful for the assistance of the company's Managing Director, Andrew McGeachin

My agent, Mandy Little, has kept me focused on the task in hand, and I profited considerably in the early stages of the book from the help and advice of Fiona Shoop. My old friend, Julian Bene, read much of the text and tried – possibly not always successfully – to weed out my mistakes. Those that remain, of course, are my responsibility alone.

But the greatest thanks of all, of course, go to my wife Penny, who has shared in the book from the start, and I suspect has enjoyed it as much as I have – and, as ever, to Dr Tim Littlewood and his NHS team at the John Radcliffe Hospital, Oxford.

Chapter One

What is Poetry?

Poetry and prose

MOST PEOPLE understand that there is a difference between poetry and prose – but they have struggled for centuries, from Aristotle to the present day, to say exactly what it is.

Nobody has succeeded.

The *Oxford English Dictionary* starts by saying that poetry is 'the art or work of the poet', which is less than helpful. It goes on to suggest that it is 'composition in verse or metrical language', which might take us a little further, if only we could be sure what verse is. So perhaps it is better to leave the dictionary, and turn to the poets themselves: several of them have tried to define poetry, and surely they should know what it is that they are writing?

William Wordsworth said it was 'the spontaneous overflow of powerful feelings', which seems to suggest confusingly that if you sit down and think about what you are writing, you don't end up with a poem. The American poet Robert Frost, trying to put his finger on the uniqueness and irreducibility of a poem, said that poetry is 'what gets lost in translation'; Edgar Allan Poe, that it is 'the rhythmical creation of beauty in words', which presumably puts paid to the description of blood 'gargling from the froth-corrupted lungs' in Wilfred Owen's *Dulce et Decorum Est*. Emily Dickinson said, 'If I feel physically as if the top of my head were taken off, I know that is poetry'; and Dylan Thomas covered pretty well all the bases when he declared that it was 'what makes me laugh or cry or yawn, what makes my toenails twinkle, what makes me want to do this or that or nothing.'

After all those definitions, it's almost a relief to come to T.S. Eliot, who said: 'Genuine poetry can communicate before it is understood' – so perhaps trying to understand it at all is just a waste of time?

The Line

The problem with trying to reach a cut-and-dried definition is that the difference between poetry and prose is very largely one of degree. Is the

King James Bible, for instance, poetry or prose? We have all read poetic prose, and we can imagine a (bad) prosaic poem. Fixing the point at which one becomes the other is like deciding when dark blue becomes light blue, or trying to nail steam to the wall. But if, despite the difficulties, we are determined to sort out which is which, maybe none of the efforts of the poets and wise men has come as close to a really useful working definition as the little girl in just her second year at school, who observed that poetry was easier to read because the lines are shorter.

She didn't realise it, but she had identified one important fact: the line is the crucial unit of poetry. You can break up *Pride and Prejudice* or *War and Peace* however you want: print them out in a single line along a long strip of paper, and you will still have an edition of Jane Austen's or Leo Tolstoy's novel. But Shakespeare's sonnets, or *Paradise Lost*, or one of Benjamin Zephaniah's *Vegan Poems*, demand to be set out, and read, and understood in lines.

Of course, there are other features of poetry which usually distinguish it from prose: it may rhyme, for instance, and there is generally a metrical pattern to the lines – although poems written in free verse, or *vers libre*, like, for example, those of Walt Whitman, may aim to catch the rhythms and tenor of ordinary speech rather than follow any accepted verse form. Almost always, this handling of rhythm and the stresses on individual words and syllables is a crucial part of the poet's art, and understanding the skill with which a poem accommodates the specific demands of a particular verse-form may be an important part of appreciating its merit.

An intense language

But more than anything, poetry is about language, and the way that it is used. Generally, whether they are printed on a sign saying 'Keep off the grass' or in Bertrand Russell's *History of Western Philosophy*, we use words to pass on information: poetry is different.

Thomas Hardy's famous poem, *The Convergence of the Twain*, for instance, written after the sinking of the *Titanic*, tells us that the ship is lying on the bottom of the sea, that an iceberg was formed long before the ship set out on its journey, and that the two collided. If that were all, our response might be 'So what? We knew all that.' In addition, though, the poem tells us that the ship's furnaces have mysteriously turned into musical instruments, that fish swim around the wreckage and speak to each other, and that some mystical character called the Spinner of the Years instructed ship and iceberg to collide. We haven't heard any of that before, but in a literal sense, it's all nonsense: so what is true in the poem is not new, and what is new is not true.

But this is a poem, not a newspaper report, and Hardy uses the language in it to evoke powerful emotions that we will all recognise, if only we will let the poem speak to us. The sea forces its way through the wrecked engines, making the huge furnaces vibrate like lyres; sea worms, horrible to our eyes, crawl over the mirrors without any thought of the wealthy passengers who once admired themselves in them; we can imagine the fish wondering how such strange artefacts come to be at the bottom of the sea. And then Hardy's final line 'And consummation comes, and jars two hemispheres' reveals where the poem has been remorselessly heading all the time: the collision is the culmination of forces which are infinitely greater than anything controllable by man, and which have been building unseen for years. That word 'consummation' suggests a sense of purpose, of mysterious intent; it has echoes of "consume", but it also stirs in us thoughts of the consummation of a marriage: there is, it seems, a mystical sense in which the disaster was meant to happen. In any case, the shuddering crash of ship and iceberg sends shivers through both Europe and America. (To Hardy, clearly, early Twentieth Century Europe and America represented the two halves of the important world: there is material for a whole new book in the way that contemporary assumptions and prejudices are reflected in poetry.)

There will be many other interpretations of this poem – one of the marks of great poetry is that it can be interpreted and re-interpreted by different readers, and even by the same reader coming to it at different times – but this is certainly one. Instead of simply reporting what happened – which we probably knew already – Hardy is telling a story of how Man's ingenuity overreached itself, of how the natural world has swallowed the great ship without trace, and of how, frighteningly, all this might have been decreed by Fate from the start.

So what is poetry?

The Twentieth Century American poet Archibald MacLeish famously declared in his poem *Ars Poetica* that 'A poem should not mean / But be' by which he meant that it cannot be paraphrased: if a prose version could explain the meaning of a poem, then the poet would have written a prose version. It cannot, as Robert Frost observed, be translated either: the most successful translations from other languages and cultures – Dryden's translations of Horace, Ted Hughes's version of Ovid, Seamus Heaney's *Beowulf,* or Simon Armitage's *Sir Gawain and the Green Knight* – are poems in their own right, which give a flavour of the original.

A sensitive command of rhythm and metre or the use of devices such as rhyme, alliteration and assonance adds to the overall effect of a poem by evoking a particular atmosphere, or linking individual words or phrases to each other. In *The Convergence of the Twain*, each stanza is bound together by rhyme, while alliteration and assonance, in phrases such as 'shadowy, silent distance' with the sibilant sound of an icy wind, create a sense of the eerie remoteness of the iceberg. But poetry is essentially language used with the greatest possible intensity, with an awareness of the precise meaning and the possible connotations of every word, and with the intent of stirring emotion within the reader. It's a long way from a complete definition – but it's about as far as we can go.

Chapter Two

The Growth of English Poetry

The Beginnings

THE HISTORY of poetry goes back far beyond books and manu-scripts: the *Iliad* and the *Odyssey*, for instance, which we now think of as the poems of Homer, were passed down orally for generations before being written down sometime in the Sixth Century BC. Some 1,400 years later, around the Eighth Century AD, bards were similarly performing the 3,000 lines of *Beowulf*, generally considered to be the first great poem composed in England.

Its story of self-sacrifice, heroism in battle and violent death belongs recognisably in an epic tradition that stretches from Homer through Milton's *Paradise Lost* in the Seventeenth Century and Walter Scott's *The Lay of the Last Minstrel* in the Nineteenth, and some scholars believe that the unknown poet may even have read Virgil or other classical models. However, though *Beowulf* and the other surviving fragments of Old English poetry may have been composed in England, they were not in English: their Anglo-Saxon language is incomprehensible to a modern English speaker.

So, too, are other early poems such as William Langland's *Piers Plowman*, which like *Beowulf* is notable for the alliteration that bind the lines together, and even Geoffrey Chaucer's famous *Canterbury Tales*. These Fourteenth Century poems were written down in what is now known as Middle English, but oral poetry remained a powerful con-temporary influence: many of the traditional ballads that were collected centuries later originate from around this time.

Poetry we can read today

The development of printing in the late Fifteenth Century began to fix an authoritative version of the language, and, give or take the odd unfamiliar word and the strange spelling, the poetry of the next hundred years, such as Edmund Spenser's *The Faerie Queene*, is readily intelligible today. The Sixteenth and Seventeenth Centuries, which included the great flowering

5

of the Elizabethan age, saw an outpouring of poetry that is still considered among the greatest in the language. Many of the Elizabethan poets, like William Shakespeare and Christopher Marlowe, were dramatists by profession who wrote for a wide audience, mixing learned and aristocratic themes and language with rumbustious and earthy vulgarity in much the same way as Chaucer had done. This became an important characteristic of English literature.

Other poets were high-born figures whose work was intended primarily to be circulated by hand around the Court. Spenser was awarded a pension by Queen Elizabeth, and poets such as Sir Thomas Wyatt and Sir Philip Sidney pursued glittering diplomatic and military careers. Their measured and courtly lyrical poetry was the mark of a gentleman of standing. That is not to say that they were careless amateurs, or in any way ill-prepared as poets: the Elizabethan age also saw a fascination with the techniques of poetry. The blank verse – unrhymed iambic pentameters – that was characteristic of Shakespeare's plays first appeared around this time, and Wyatt and Henry Howard, Earl of Surrey, began experimenting with new verse forms from Italy such as the sonnet.

The Wits of the Seventeenth Century

This intellectual attitude towards poetry reached its peak early in the Seventeenth Century, with the so-called Metaphysical Poets. This description, first used by Samuel Johnson a hundred years later, is now less popular because it disguises important differences between individual poets such as John Donne, Andrew Marvell, George Herbert, and Thomas Traherne, but it does reflect their common interest in science, philosophy, and disputation. They were best known for their extravagant wit and for the imaginative and carefully drawn out similes or conceits which characterise much of their poetry – Donne's *A Valediction, Forbidding Mourning*, for instance, compares the poet and his lover to the two legs of a pair of compasses, and Marvell's *To His Coy Mistress* pictures his love as a vast and slow-growing vegetable. Many of their poems were about love, but they also focused on matters of religion, particularly in Donne's so-called Holy Sonnets.

Another group of poets around the same time, including such figures as Robert Herrick and Richard Lovelace, became known as the Cavalier Poets because of their support for King Charles in the Civil Wars. Rather than the subtle wit and convoluted logic of the Metaphysical Poets, the Cavalier Poets wrote simple, direct lyric poetry, often concerned with love, loyalty, and sensuality. It was the relaxed and extravagant verse of a self-consciously aristocratic elite.

The greatest poet of the age, John Milton, fitted into the lyrical tradition with such works as *Lycidas, L'Allegro* and *II Penseroso*, and also into the pattern of religious poetry – his famous epic, *Paradise Lost*, retold the story of Adam and Eve. However, he remained a passionate supporter of the Parliamentary side in the Civil Wars, and a loyal public servant under Cromwell. Poems such as his sonnet *On the Late Massacre in Piedmont* reflect the fact that religion was inextricably bound up with politics.

The Eighteenth Century – Looking Back to the Past

Milton, who died in poverty in 1674, 14 years after the Restoration of Charles II, was a noted scholar of Greek and Latin poetry, and this admiration for Classical literature was a key element of the Augustan Age which lasted from the Restoration to the middle of the Eighteenth Century. Poets of this period, such as John Dryden, Jonathan Swift, John Gay, and particularly Alexander Pope, consciously compared themselves with the Roman writers of the time of Caesar Augustus. This, the poetry of the Age of Enlightenment, was the literary expression of a philosophical commitment to the idea of a rational and comprehensible universe.

Stylistically, the Augustans favoured tightly controlled and regular verse forms – this was the age of the heroic couplet – and valued clarity and decorum. Dryden's prose work *An Essay of Dramatic Poesy* and Pope's long poem *An Essay on Criticism* set out this philosophy explicitly. However, the focus on classical models also encouraged the development of satiric writing, with mock epics such as Pope's *Dunciad* and *The Rape of the Lock*, Dryden's *MacFlecknoe*, or, on the stage, Gay's *The Beggar's Opera*.

The Romantic Imagination

The publication in 1798 of the first edition of *Lyrical Ballads*, by William Wordsworth and Samuel Taylor Coleridge, was one of the most important dates in English literature, marking the start of the Romantic

7

era which has influenced poetry ever since. The two young poets, still in their twenties, explicitly rejected what they called the 'gaudiness and inane phraseology' of Eighteenth Century literature, and declared that their poetry – and by implication, *all* poetry – would be founded on feeling and imagination, not restraint and rationality. Instead of the models of Classical literature, they would focus on 'natural' man: Wordsworth's *Prelude* had as its hero not the noble man of action who was familiar from traditional epic poetry, but the poet himself, in all his complexity, suffering, and occasional inadequacy. Instead of the sonorous, Latinate style and poetic diction of the Augustans, Wordsworth and Coleridge announced their ambition to write in 'the very language of men'.

It was a major change of direction, even though later Eighteenth Century poets such as Thomas Gray and the so-called 'Graveyard Poets' had already begun to write poetry that concentrated on their own feelings and emotions, and the poet and painter William Blake had pointed the way towards political radicalism in verse. The Romantic poets – notably John Keats, Percy Bysshe Shelley, and Lord Byron, as well as Wordsworth and Coleridge – echoed similar literary and philosophical movements in several European countries, responding to the revolutions in America and France, to wars of independence in Poland, Spain, and Greece, and to the dehumanising effects of the industrial revolution. They concentrated on the magnificence of nature rather than the more studied intellectual beauty that had concerned the Augustans; they committed themselves politically to the struggle for liberty rather than the promotion of order.

The Poetry of the Victorians

The one-time leader of the Romantic literary revolution, William Wordsworth, who lived on until 1850, was widely derided later in his life for having abandoned his earlier radicalism, but in fact the literary landscape as a whole changed with the early deaths of most of the leading Romantics. The fascination that the *Lyrical Ballads* showed for nature and the imagination of the individual survives in much of the poetry of the later Victorians such as Alfred Lord Tennyson, Robert Browning, and Matthew Arnold, but the earlier political radicalism was largely doused.

In little over 30 years, from 1809 to 1842, English poetry travelled from the young Wordsworth's exuberant welcome for the French Revolution,

'Bliss was it in that dawn to be alive,
But to be young was very heaven,'

to Robert Browning's regretful 'Never glad confident morning again'.

Poets were inspired by the rapid social and technological changes of the time, but they also started to look backwards again. This time, though, many of them took their models and themes from Medieval times, rather than the Classical age as the Augustans had done – Tennyson's *Idylls of the King* was a cycle of 12 narrative poems telling the story of King Arthur and his Knights of the Round Table, and Browning wrote several dramatic monologues set in the Medieval age. But this renewed interest in the past was particularly evident in the later Victorian poets such as Dante Gabriel Rossetti and Algernon Charles Swinburne, who allied themselves with the painters of the Pre Raphaelite Brotherhood. Their moody, idealised view of the past, often with a thinly-veiled sexuality, was bitterly attacked by outraged critics as 'the Fleshly School of Poetry', but continued to influence English writing into the Twentieth Century. Ernest Dowson and Oscar Wilde are just two members of the so-called Decadent Movement who sought to struggle against the materialistic preoccupations of industrialised society with a lush, sensuous poetry that can be traced back to the Pre Raphaelites.

War Poets and Georgians

Among many poets around the late Nineteenth and early Twentieth Century, there was a renewed awareness of the rural traditions of the different parts of Britain. Many of Thomas Hardy's short lyrics dealt with the ancient stories and customs of his Wessex homeland, while poets such as 'AE' Russell, and most notably William Butler Yeats were fired by a passion for the ancient Celtic language and literature of Ireland. In Scotland, this had started at least a hundred years earlier, with the poetry of Robert Burns, James Hogg, and Sir Walter Scott, but by 1920, the poet Hugh MacDiarmid suggested that a new generation of Twentieth Century Scottish poets had brought about a fresh 'Scottish Renaissance'.

In 1912, two years after the accession of King George V, the first of five volumes appeared with the title *Georgian Poetry*. The collections, which continued to appear over the next 10 years, were originally planned by a group of poets led by Rupert Brooke and Harold Monro, and also concentrated largely on the countryside and nature. They featured verse in highly traditional forms, with consciously poetic language. The Georgian Poets, who also included W.H. Davies, John Masefield, Walter de la Mare, and John Drinkwater, were extremely popular up to and during the First World War – the early work of the war poet Wilfred Owen was heavily influenced by Georgian ideas and techniques – but the backward-looking idealism which characterised much of their work was wholly unfitted to reflect the horror and disillusionment of those poets who experienced the slaughter of the trenches.

War had always been a subject for poetry, and the heavy casualties of the Boer War had inspired poets such as Thomas Hardy to write about the death and suffering of individual soldiers. But no one had ever described the reality of modern conflict with the sickening realism and uncompromising physical detail of Owen, Siegfried Sassoon, Isaac Rosenberg and the other poets of the First World War. The appearance of their work during and shortly after the war – Owen's posthumous collection was published in 1920 – not only shocked readers with the ruthless descriptions of trench warfare, but also provided a model for a new, realistic, and almost aggressively 'unpoetic' poetry.

This challenge to the Georgian establishment was confirmed and reinforced by the publication of T.S. Eliot's collection *Prufrock and Other Observations* in 1917, an event which, together with the appearance of *The Waste Land* five years later, had an effect comparable with the appearance of Wordsworth and Coleridge's *Lyrical Ballads*. English poetry had undergone another sudden radical change.

The Modernists and After

In fact, just as Blake, Thomas Gray, and other late Eighteenth Century poets had prefigured the revolution of the Romantics, so a number of poets known as Imagists, including T.E. Hulme and William Carlos Williams, had already demonstrated some of the features of Modernism in their work.

Eliot's poetry, however, marks the defining moment of the early Modernist movement. Like Ezra Pound, James Joyce, and W.B. Yeats in his later years, he abandoned the traditional structure of much Victorian and Georgian poetry, with its logical narrative and exposition, in favour of the presentation of a succession of poetic images – a technique that developed into the so-called 'stream of consciousness' typified in prose by Joyce's novel *Ulysses*. Instead of trying to represent the way that people spoke, Modernist poetry increasingly sought to reflect the way that they thought.

Modernism continued to influence English poetry, encouraging poets to explore new and innovative rhythms and metrical patterns, to experiment in their use of language, and to express themselves through images. However, the traditional verse forms of Thomas Hardy also provided a lasting model, particularly for the Thirties Poets, led by W.H. Auden, and, later, for the 1950s poets such as Philip Larkin, D.J. Enright, and John Wain, who became leading figures in a group known as the Movement.

It is impossible to see yet how contemporary poetry will fit into this pattern. Among the effects of various changes in society such as mass immigration, the growth of television, the internet, and the ubiquitous music industry, the lasting influence of the Modernists can still be seen in the concentration of many poets on the overwhelming importance of the image. The Romantic idea of the importance of the individual clearly survives, and poets such as Ted Hughes and Seamus Heaney have continued the tradition of focusing on the natural world. More than 12 centuries after the Anglo Saxon bards were reciting *Beowulf*, the changes and developments in English poetry are still continuing.

Chapter Three

The Poet's Art

JOHN KEATS, probably the most magical writer of lyric poetry in the whole of English literature, seemed to have no doubts. Poetry, he said, should come 'as naturally as the leaves to a tree'. But that doesn't mean that the writing of poetry is a purely instinctive act: a cry of anguish or a scream of delight is not the same as a poem.

To enjoy poetry, it helps to understand something about its mechanics – about the way that the rhythms and stresses of the words that the poet uses help to create the effect that he seeks, and the way that different types of metre shape the lines that he writes. Pope, in his *Essay on Criticism*, had this to say about the poet's art:

> 'True ease in writing comes from art, not chance
> As those move easiest who have learn'd to dance.'

In Greek or Latin verse, metre is determined by the pattern of long and short syllables, but in English it depends entirely on the weight or emphasis that is put on each syllable – on its *stress*. As in learning to dance, the pupil has to learn where to put his feet, so in writing poetry, the poet has to learn where to put his stress. Even so-called 'free verse', which has no strict metre, has to consider where the stress goes in normal speech, and any piece of formal poetry will generally conform to one of several different metrical patterns.

The Four English Metres

Most English poetry is written in one of four metres – *iambic, trochaic, dactylic* or *anapaestic*.

In the *pentameter*, each line has five *feet*, or repeated patterns of stresses; an *iamb* is a foot composed of an unstressed syllable followed by a stressed one; and so an *iambic pentameter*, which is the most common metre used in English, is a line composed of five iambic feet. Most of Shakespeare's plays are written in iambic pentameters (*blank verse* is simply unrhymed iambic pentameters): 'The **barge** / she **sat** / in, **like** / a **burn**/ish'd **throne** . . .'. They are also used in sonnets, heroic couplets, and many other verse forms. It is almost impossible to imagine English poetry without the iambic pentameter.

Turn an iambic foot around, and you have a *trochee*, one in which a single stressed syllable is followed by a stressed one – the word *tiger* is an example. Put it in a line of poetry, and you might have William Blake's '**Ty**ger / **ty**ger / **burn**ing / *bright* . . .' where each line is completed by a single extra stressed syllable.

The other two types of metre each have three syllables to a foot. The *dactyl* has one stressed syllable followed by two unstressed ones. Take Tennyson's *The Charge of the Light Brigade*, for instance:

'**Half** a league, | **half** a league | **half** a league | **on** ward . . .'

Just as the trochee is the reverse of the iamb, so the *anapaest* is the mirror-image of the dactyl – two unstressed syllables followed by one stressed. The urgent, ominous effect is famously exemplified in Byron's *The Destruction of Sennacherib*:

'The As**syr** | ian came **down** | like the **wolf** | on the **fold** . . .'

Bending the rules

These descriptions might make poetry sound very mechanical – as if Pope, in his advice about dancing, were setting out precise sets of steps that writers ought to take to produce poetry. It's not like that: the poet's art lies in the way that he *uses* the different metres. Pope went on to say:

"Tis not enough no harshness gives offence,
The sound must seem an echo to the sense.'

Of course, the poet must choose the right metre for the type of poem that is being written, like Byron whipping up excitement with his hurrying anapaests. Beyond that, though, he needs to adapt the metre to his purposes. Whether it is Shakespeare varying the lines in his blank verse, or Keats reversing the iamb in the first foot of his sonnet *On First Looking into Chapman's Homer* so that the stress falls on the first word, not the second and leaving the sixth syllable (in) unstressed – '**Much** have / I **trav** / ell'd in / the **realms** / of **gold** ...' – the poet is constantly shifting and adjusting the stress patterns in the line. It is a matter of using his ear to listen to the music of the line – but you have to know the rules to be able to bend them.

Verse forms and genres

From the 15,000 or so lines of the *Odyssey* to the tiny perfection of a two-line epigram, from the tight construction of a formal sonnet to the wandering exuberance of a traditional ballad, poetry takes an almost limitless variety of forms. The choice of form depends on what the poet is trying to say – Homer could hardly have told the detailed stories of the Trojan wars and the wanderings of Odysseus in a 14-line sonnet.

THE EPIC

In a sense, at least as far as western European poetry is concerned, everything has come from the epic. But though Homer's two great poems provide a convenient starting point for European literature as a whole, they also started a tradition of specifically epic poetry. Describing the adventures of a heroic figure or group of figures from either history or mythology, and often involving similes and descriptions which may stretch over many lines, the epic has been instrumental in diffusing creation myths about a variety of different cultures. Ancient Greeks saw their history reflected in the *Odyssey* and *Iliad* and Virgil gave the Romans a noble past in the *Aeneid*, while the anonymous *Beowulf* did the same for the Anglo Saxons. Milton's *Paradise Lost* is a Christian epic of the Seventeenth Century, and *Idylls of the King*, by Tennyson, a romanticised Medieval epic from the Nineteenth. Epic poetry is less common in modern times, although Derek Walcott's *Omeros* might be seen as a Twentieth Century epic centred on the Caribbean island of St Lucia.

THE BALLAD

The ballad is another ancient verse form, dating in Britain from the Medieval period. It generally tells a story, and was often set to music, with repeated lines and choruses. Essentially an oral form in origin, when it was written down it was often set out in four-line stanzas or quatrains. Traditional ballads, gathered together enthusiastically in the Seventeenth and Eighteenth Centuries, provided a framework for poems such as Samuel Taylor Coleridge's *The Rime of the Ancient Mariner*, although later examples, such as Oscar Wilde's *Ballad of Reading Gaol*, may be much more sophisticated than their traditional, anonymous models.

THE SONNET

The sonnet, a 14-line poem, generally with a fixed rhyme-scheme and often with a break between the first eight lines (the *octave*) and the final six (the *sestet*), was introduced into English from Italy during the Sixteenth Century. Thomas Wyatt, Edmund Spenser, Shakespeare and Milton are just a few of the notable poets of the Sixteenth and Seventeenth Centuries who produced sonnets in iambic pentameters that conformed to the pattern, although they had different rhyme schemes. Sonnets remain among the most popular types of short formal poetry, although modern writers such as Carol Ann Duffy, Seamus Heaney, or Louis MacNeice may bend the rules almost to breaking point.

THE ODE

For the Ancient Greeks, who devised the form, the ode was a musical composition, arranged in three sections. Today, it is used to describe a rhyming poem written in homage to an individual, such as Andrew Marvell's *Horatian Ode Upon Cromwell's Return from Ireland*, or to a particular quality such as beauty as exemplified to the poet by some thought or object – think of John Keats's *Ode on a Grecian Urn* or *Ode to Autumn*, or Shelley's *Ode to the West Wind*.

THE VILLANELLE

The villanelle, introduced into English in the late Nineteenth Century from French and Italian models, has a very flexible metre, but a fixed and complex scheme of rhymes and repetitions over its 19 lines. The poem is arranged in five three-line stanzas (*tercets*) and a concluding quatrain. The first and third lines are repeated as a final couplet; and in addition, the first line is repeated as the final line of the second and fourth tercet, and the third line as the final line of the third and fifth. Dylan Thomas's *Do Not Go Gentle into That Good Night* is a famous modern example, and there are others by Oscar Wilde, W.H. Auden, Vernon Scannell, and Seamus Heaney.

THE HAIKU

Japanese poets have been writing haiku for several hundred years, but the form was adapted for English – a three-line, unrhymed poem in which the lines have five, seven, and five syllables respectively – early in the Twentieth Century. It reflected the contemporary concentration of the Imagist movement on short poems which focused on a single memorable image, and remains a popular avant-garde form.

FREE VERSE

Free verse is 'free' in the sense that it is unrhymed, and not bound by any of the metrical conventions of formal poetry – but the poet T.S. Eliot warned in his essay, *The Music of Poetry*: 'No verse is free for the man who wants to do a good job.'

Some critics trace its ancestry back to the alliterative poetry of Medieval times, others to the Bible, and some even back to the earliest poets of ancient Greek, but in the modern age, the American poet Walt Whitman is generally considered the first consistent writer of free verse. A glance at a couple of his lines:

> 'When I read the book, the biography famous
> And is this then (said I) what the author calls a man's life?'

it is clear that rhythm and stress patterns remain important, even though they cannot easily be analysed. The same is true of other poets who have written in free verse – D.H. Lawrence, Ezra Pound, or William Carlos Williams.

The truth is that poetry – writing it or reading it – is always a mixture of originality and tradition, of inspiration and sheer hard work. As Gerard Manley Hopkins wrote:

'No wonder of it. Sheer plod makes plough down sillion
Shine, and blue-bleak embers, ah my dear,
Fall, gall themselves, and gash gold-vermilion.'

There are no easy answers, and no short cuts.

Chapter Four

The Poets

Homer (c. Eighth or Ninth Century BC)

THE POSSIBLY mythical author of the *Iliad* and probably the *Odyssey*, the epic stories of the siege of Troy and the subsequent wanderings of Odysseus, is generally accepted as the first poet in western literature. Virtually nothing is known about his life – even his supposed blindness is based on tradition, with no historical evidence to confirm the story. One modern theory is that, while he may have composed, rather than writing down, the *Iliad*, the *Odyssey* could have been the work of another poet several decades later, inspired by and possibly imitating the earlier poem. Both poems are likely to have been changed and adapted by other wandering poets as they were handed down orally for several generations before being written down. However, there is no doubt of their influence on western culture: western poetry, the theatre, and the novel all include the *Iliad* and the *Odyssey* among their earliest literary antecedents.

Sappho (c.620 BC–c.570 BC)

There are many legends about the Greek poet Sappho, but almost nothing is known for certain about her life, although she is believed to have lived on the Greek island of Lesbos in the late Seventh or early Sixth Century BC. Her surviving fragmentary works were first collected some three hundred years after her death. They are mainly simple and direct lyrics about love, and are the first poems in Western culture supposed to have been written by a woman.

Virgil (70 BC–19 BC)

Publius Virgilius Maro (Virgil) is generally considered the greatest Roman poet. Drawing on his personal experience as the son of a farmer, his pastorals (the *Eclogues* and *Georgics*) offered practical advice on farming and rural life, but his most influential work is his great patriotic epic about the supposed origins of the Roman people, the *Aeneid*. This poem, unfinished at Virgil's death, traces the wanderings of its hero, Aeneas, from the fall of Troy to his defeat of the Italian tribes. Virgil was seen by later ages as the archetypal poet and seer, and was chosen by Dante as his guide through the underworld in his *Divine Comedy*.

Horace (65 BC–8 BC)

The Roman poet Quintus Horatius Flaccus (Horace) – the son of a former slave – was one of a group of writers during the so-called 'Golden Age' of the Emperor Augustus. His *Odes*, written in four books, are lyrical poems loosely based on Greek models, while his *Satires* and *Epistles* introduced a new irony into Latin literature. The works of Horace, particularly his *Ars Poetica* (*The Art of Poetry*), a treatise on how poetry should be written and appreciated, have been extremely influential in the development of English literature, notably during the Seventeenth and Eighteenth Centuries.

Ovid (43 BC–17 AD)

Publius Ovidius Naso (Ovid) wrote poetry in several styles and genres including: love elegies, the *Amores*; imaginary letters, *Heroides*; didactic verse about the art of love, *Ars Amatoria*; and narrative verse, *Metamorphoses*. Scenes and stories from the latter collection were copied by painters and writers from the Renaissance onwards, including Chaucer and Shakespeare. However, some of Ovid's greatest poetry was written after his exile by the Emperor Augustus to the Black Sea, where he wrote the *Tristia* (*Griefs*) and *Epistulae ex Ponto* (*Letters from the Black Sea*), a series of nostalgic elegies about his lost life in Rome.

The Beowulf poet (c. Eighth Century)

The Anglo-Saxon epic *Beowulf* is believed to have been composed as early as the Eighth Century. Nothing is known about its anonymous author, and the poem may well have been transmitted orally for generations before being set down by two scribes in the only surviving manuscript version sometime in the Eleventh Century. It is set in Scandinavia, and tells the story of the titanic struggles against various monsters of its eponymous hero, who was a prince of the Scandinavian Geat people. Although it is written in Anglo-Saxon, and is therefore incomprehensible to a speaker of modern English, it is often considered not just as an important historical source of information about life under the Saxons, but also as the first major poem in a European vernacular language, and one of the earliest triumphs of literature in England.

Dante Alighieri (1265–1321)

The Italian poet Dante Alighieri was active in the turbulent political life of Florence at the start of the Fourteenth Century, but was banished from the city when a rival faction seized power, and spent much of his life as a wandering exile in the Italian city states. His greatest work is the monumental epic *La Divina Commedia* (*The Divine Comedy*) (c.1307–1321), which he finished shortly before his death. The three books of the poem, *Inferno*, *Purgatorio*, and *Paradiso* describe visits to Hell, Purgatory, and Paradise respectively, with the Roman poet Virgil acting as Dante's guide in the first two books, and his idealised lover Beatrice in the third. Dante also wrote *La Vita Nuova* (The New Life), a sequence of 31 lyrics describing his passionate love for Beatrice and his hopes for salvation, as well as a number of individual lyric poems and philosophical and political treatises.

The Gawain poet (c. Fourteenth Century)

The 2,500-line Fourteenth Century epic, *Sir Gawain and the Green Knight*, like *Beowulf*, survives in a single manuscript, and is the work of an otherwise unknown poet. It is written in Middle English, an early combination of Anglo-Saxon and Norman French, and tells the story of the adventure of Sir Gawain, one of King Arthur's knights, in his quest for the miraculous Green Knight. Its creator is also widely supposed to have written three religious lyrics, *Pearl*, *Cleanness*, and *Patience*, which are recorded on the same manuscript as *Sir Gawain*.

Geoffrey Chaucer (c.1343–1400)

The works of Geoffrey Chaucer are not easily accessible in the original to the modern reader because of changes in the written and spoken language since the Fourteenth Century, but his poems, particularly his unfinished masterpiece, *The Canterbury Tales* (possibly c.1380–1400), have had an immense influence on English literature over the last six centuries.

It is only in the last hundred and fifty years that there has been any agreement about exactly which poems are definitely attributable to Chaucer, but his first known major work, *The Book of the Duchess* (c.1370), is an elegy for Blanche, Duchess of Lancaster, the first wife of Chaucer's friend and patron, John of Gaunt. Other poems which followed during the next two decades include *The House of Fame* (c.1379); *The Parliament of Fowls* (probably early 1380s), a study of the nature of love in the form of a dream-poem in which the birds meet to choose their mates on St. Valentine's Day; and *Troilus and Criseyde* (probably late 1380s), an 8,000-line version of the tragic love story set against the background of the Trojan War and shot through with philosophical and religious thoughts about determinism and free will and sexual love as compared to the love of God.

Around 1359, Chaucer had spent time in France as a soldier in Edward III's army and later as a prisoner of the French, during which period he became acquainted with French allegorical poetry, and later, pursuing a successful career as a Government servant, he travelled on diplomatic business to Flanders, France, and Italy. It is likely that on these latter journeys he would have studied the works of European writers such as Dante, Petrarch, and Boccaccio, and his introduction of French, Italian, and classical influences into his poetry – *Troilus and Criseyde* was based on an earlier work by Boccaccio – was an important innovation for English Literature.

Despite the political upheavals of the time, including the Peasants' Revolt of 1381, Chaucer's government career continued to prosper. He was appointed to a highly profitable role in collecting taxes at the Port of London, elected to Parliament, created a justice of the peace, and given the job of Richard II's clerk of works, with responsibility for the repair and maintenance of royal buildings. Later, he was presented with royal gifts and pensions by both King Richard and the successor who overthrew him in 1399, Henry IV. Because of these marks of royal favour, he is sometimes considered the first Poet Laureate.

In his early forties, Chaucer had started work on *The Canterbury Tales*, which uses the convention of a pilgrimage to bring together 31 characters who tell each other stories on their way to the shrine of St. Thomas à Becket at Canterbury. From the Knight to the humble Ploughman, the pilgrims make up a cross-section of Chaucer's world, although there are no aristocrats and no members of the lowest orders of society. Each individual story is carefully related to the background and character of the pilgrim who tells it. The stories – two of them in prose – embrace various literary genres, including the courtly romance of the Knight; the coarse, crude, and cynical tales of the Miller and the Cook; the beast fable of the Nun's Priest, and the religious miracle story of the Second Nun.

Despite containing some 17,000 lines of prose and verse, the poem is actually considerably shorter than the version Chaucer had planned to write, although the final tale, by the Parson, ends with a farewell from the poet. However, there are only 24 tales in the series, and the original plan was to have each pilgrim tell four, adding up, at least in theory, to a total of over a hundred and twenty.

But the poem as it stands – written, like almost all of Chaucer's work, in the rough and sometimes bawdy conversational English of ordinary people, rather than the aristocratic French of the aristocracy – is not only acknowledged as a masterpiece of its time, but also considered the original pattern for a distinctly English mixture of vernacular language and courtly style which has remained popular ever since. Several writers, including Shakespeare, Pope, and Dryden, have borrowed or adapted tales from Chaucer, but the influence of his style and his use of the vernacular has permeated English Literature.

The character of the narrator is also a significant innovation. The Chaucer who tells the story is supposedly part of the pilgrimage –

> 'In Southwerk at the Tabard as I lay,
> Redy to wenden on my pilgrimage,'

he says – and he is presented as a wide-eyed, trusting, and naïve observer. But his shrewd comments note the foibles and hypocrisies of the different pilgrims, from the Monk who prefers hunting to sacred texts to the Prioress whose brooch with the words *Amor vincit omnia* (Love conquers all) suggests that her interests are not wholly theological. Only the Knight, the Parson, and the Ploughman, the representatives of military, religious, and civil life, are presented as entirely sincere and upright.

When he died, Chaucer was presumably still writing tales to be incorporated into the series. Little is known about the final years of his life, although it seems clear that he remained in favour with the new king, Henry IV, after the overthrow of Richard II. The date of his death is usually considered to be October 25 1400, just over a year after Henry's coronation, but this is taken from the engraving on a memorial in Westminster Abbey which was erected more than a century after his death, and so may be inaccurate. Whatever the precise date, however, he may be considered to be the first poet to have been buried in Poets' Corner in the Abbey, where the graves and memorials of his successors – other writers from Edmund Spenser to William Shakespeare, John Dryden, and Lord Byron – now stand.

John Skelton (c.1460–c.1529)

John Skelton, a poet and scholar, served King Henry VII as a courtier and Poet Laureate in the late Fifteenth Century, and around 1500 was appointed tutor to the future King Henry VIII. Among his surviving works are bitterly satirical verses, such as *Speke Parot* (1521), *'Ware the Hawke* (late 1490s) and *Colyn Cloute* (1522) about abuses in the Church, a triumphal song *Against the Scottes* (1513) to celebrate the English victory at the Battle of Flodden, and a light-hearted, ironic poem, *Phillyp Sparowe* (late 1490s) in which a young girl mourns for her pet bird. His rumbustious *The Tunning of Elinor Rumming* (c.1518), about the bawdy customers at an alehouse, helped to establish a lasting reputation for him as a lively and ribald joker. His characteristic verse form, with short lines, frequently repeated rhymes, and heavy rhythms, became known as Skeltonic.

William Dunbar (c.1456–c.1513)

William Dunbar was a poet, priest, and courtier at the Court of James IV of Scotland. Among the hundred or so poems believed to be written by him are allegories, comic poems, satires and devotional pieces. His most famous poem, written in memory of earlier Scottish poets, is an elegy focusing on the brevity of earthly life, entitled *Lament for the Makers*. It contains the repeated Latin line 'Timor mortis conturbat me' (The fear of death troubles me). Dunbar is believed to have died at the Battle of Flodden.

Sir Thomas Wyatt (1503–1542)

Sir Thomas Wyatt was a high-ranking diplomat and courtier at the Court of Henry VIII. His sonnet *Whoso list to hunt*, translated from an Italian original by Petrarch, tells of a mystical deer wearing a diamond collar engraved with the warning '*Noli me tangere (Do not touch me) for Caesar's I am*', and is often thought to refer to Anne Boleyn, who several contemporary accounts say was Wyatt's lover before she caught the King's eye. It is known that he fell from official favour, and was twice imprisoned in the Tower of London. Along with Henry Howard, Earl of Surrey, he is one of the first poets to bring the Italian sonnet form into English literature. He also wrote satires, epigrams, songs, and religious poems.

Henry Howard, Earl of Surrey (1516–1547)

Henry Howard, Earl of Surrey, a cousin of Anne Boleyn and childhood playmate of the King's illegitimate son Henry Fitzroy, Duke of Richmond, was a soldier and an aristocrat at the Court of Henry VIII. His famous poem *Prisoned in Windsor*, written while he was in prison as a suspected traitor, recalls his childhood at the Royal palace. Along with Sir Thomas Wyatt, he is considered one of the most important founders of English Renaissance poetry. He wrote in the new Italian sonnet form and, in his translation of two books of Virgil's *Aeneid*, he was also one of the first English poets to write in the unrhymed blank verse later made famous in Shakespeare's plays. Surrey was tried and executed on charges of treason. Most of his poetry, including large numbers of songs, sonnets, and love poems, was only published some 10 years after his death.

Sir Walter Ralegh (1552–1618)

Soldier, scholar, explorer, historian, courtier, and gifted lyric poet, Sir Walter Ralegh seemed to exemplify the disparate talents of the ideal Renaissance man. He was one of the first English colonisers of the New World at Roanoke Island in present day North Carolina, and a leader of the ill-fated search for El Dorado in South America. Many of his poems, such as his sonnet *Methought I saw the grave where Laura lay*, about Homer, Petrarch, and Edmund Spenser, are self-conscious literary exercises, but the overwhelming mood of Ralegh's poetry is one of nostalgic regret. He also wrote a sardonic reply to Christopher Marlowe's romantic pastoral *The Passionate Shepherd to his Love*, in which the nymph urges the shepherd to be more realistic. Although Ralegh was one of Elizabeth I's favourites, he fell out of favour under James I, and was executed after Spanish complaints about his activities in the Americas. His final poem, reportedly written the night before his execution and later found among his possessions, ends with the well-known lines 'From which earth, and grave, and dust, The Lord shall raise me up, I trust.'

Edmund Spenser (1552–1599)

Educated in London at the Merchant Taylors' School and at Cambridge University, Edmund Spenser was an ambitious courtier and servant of Queen Elizabeth I. His great epic poem, *The Faerie Queene* (1590–96), was written to glorify Elizabeth and the Tudor dynasty in an allegorical depiction of knightly chivalry. The unfinished poem, in six books with the surviving fragment of a seventh, was to have described the adventures of 12 knights representing different virtues such as temperance, chastity, and justice. It so pleased the Queen that Spenser, who had been a leading figure in the military suppression of Irish rebels, was awarded a pension for life. He is considered to be one of the greatest craftsmen of early English poetry, partly on account of his construction of the so-called Spenserian stanza, which consists of eight five-foot iambic lines followed by an iambic line of six feet. Among his other well-known works are his pastoral poems *The Shepheardes Calender* (1579) and *Colin Cloute's Come Home Againe* (1595), and his *Epithalamion* (1595), written to celebrate his marriage to Elizabeth Boyle.

John Lyly (1553/4–1606)

John Lyly was best known in his own day for his two-part prose work, *Euphues* (1578–1580), a witty discourse on the subject of love and romance, which was written in a distinctively ornate style which came to be known as Euphuism, and brought him great fame. However, he also wrote nine plays, including one, *The Woman in the Moon* (1597), in blank verse and another, *The Maid's Metamorphosis* (1600) in rhyme, as well as occasional songs such as *Cupid and my Campaspe played* (uncertain date), which are still popular. He is considered to have been an important influence on the early comedies of William Shakespeare.

Sir Philip Sidney (1554–1586)

Sir Philip Sidney's great prose work, *The Defence of Poesy*, is sometimes cited as the first work of literary criticism in English. In addition, however, this Elizabethan aristocrat, courtier, and soldier who died in battle at the age of 32, wrote pastoral verses, religious poetry, and love sonnets. His most famous work is his sonnet sequence *Astrophel and Stella* (c.1582). The sequence, a total of 108 sonnets and 11 songs, traces the course of an unhappy love affair, which fails to reach any resolution apart from a single snatched kiss while Stella is asleep. Sidney was also widely known as a friend and patron of other poets and writers. Edmund Spenser dedicated his pastoral *The Shepheardes Calender* to him, and also wrote an elegy, *Astrophel*, after Sidney was killed during fighting in the Netherlands.

Robert Greene (c.1560–1592)

The dramatist, pamphleteer, and poet Robert Greene is now best known for a supposed attack published in 1592, in which he jealously described the successful young William Shakespeare as an 'upstart Crow, beautified with our feathers … in his owne conceit the onely Shake-scene in a countrey'. He wrote eight verse plays, all published after his death, of which the most famous are *Orlando Furioso* (1594), *Friar Bacon and Friar Bungay* (1594), and *James the Fourth* (1598).

George Chapman (1560–1634)

Chapman's fame today rests largely on the admission by John Keats in his sonnet *Much have I travelled in the realms of gold* that it was Chapman's translations of Homer that first introduced him to Greek poetry. Apart from his versions of the *Iliad* and *Odyssey*, however, Chapman was a successful playwright and poet who wrote a number of plays, either alone or in collaboration, and several poems including *The Shadow of Night* (1594), a pair of philosophical poems about night and day. He also translated works by the Greek poets Musaeus and Hesiod, and by the Romans Virgil and Juvenal. Little is known about his life, except that he is believed to have served as a soldier and to have been plagued by debt. Chapman has sometimes been identified as the rival lover-poet referred to in Shakespeare's sonnets.

Michael Drayton (1563–1631)

Michael Drayton, a prolific writer of historical, descriptive, and religious verse, satires, odes, and sonnets, was strongly influenced by Edmund Spenser and William Shakespeare, as well as by classical models such as Horace and Ovid. His verses included a series of pastoral verses in the manner of Spenser entitled *Idea, the Shepherd's Garland* (1593); *Idea's Mirror* (1594), a sonnet sequence which he reworked throughout his life; and *Poems Lyric and Pastoral* (1606), a series of poems in imitation of Horace's *Odes*. His greatest interest, though, was in patriotic and historical verse: his most famous work, *Poly-Olbion* (1612–1622), more than 30,000 lines long, describes the history and geography of the separate counties of England and Wales.

Christopher Marlowe (1564–1593)

Christopher Marlowe was widely admired in Elizabethan London as a scholar and talented classicist, even though he was also known as a man of a criminal and violent disposition. In his mid-twenties, he was involved in a street brawl in which a man was killed. A few years later he was deported from the Netherlands for attempting to forge gold coins, and at the age of 29, shortly before he was due to appear before the Privy Council on unknown charges, he was killed in a fight in a Deptford tavern over an unpaid bill. He was also rumoured to be an atheist and a heretic. But he was a man of immense talent, generally considered second only to William Shakespeare as a dramatist, with plays such as *Tamburlaine the Great* (1587), *The Tragedie of Dido, Queen of Carthage* (1594), *Edward II* (1594), and *Dr Faustus* (1604) to his credit. He was also responsible for translations of poems by the Roman poets Ovid and Lucan, and an erotic narrative poem, *Hero and Leander*, which was completed by George Chapman and published in 1598. Probably his best-known poem today is the romantic pastoral lyric *The Passionate Shepherd to his Love* (1599), which was published posthumously. A reply was later written by Sir Walter Ralegh.

William Shakespeare (1564–1616)

The range of William Shakespeare's achievement and the depth of his influence are such that it is virtually impossible to appreciate the English literature of any period after the early Seventeenth Century without at least some acquaintance with his work.

His complete canon, generally agreed to include 38 plays, mainly written in blank verse, at least four narrative poems, and a sequence of 154 love sonnets, is generally accepted as being among the greatest bodies of work in the whole of western culture. A number of other plays and poems are considered to have been possibly or partly written by him, and at least two plays, mentioned in other contemporary documents, are lost.

Knowledge of his life is sketchy, although bearing in mind his humble origins in Stratford-upon-Avon, a surprising amount of detail has been established. He is known to have been the son of a successful Stratford businessman, and received a grammar school education in history and the classics that formed the basis for the immense breadth of knowledge displayed in his plays. Parish records reveal that at the age of 18 he married Anne Hathaway, from the nearby village of Shottery, and their daughter was baptised a year later, followed by twins, Hamnet and Judith, in 1585.

Little is known of his early career, although the Seventeenth Century antiquary John Aubrey suggests that he spent some time as a teacher. Most of Shakespeare's plays were not published in any reliable written form during his lifetime, and their dates are uncertain, but by 1594, with his family still in Stratford, he was gaining a reputation as a playwright and actor in London. This is the period of his early comedies, such as *The Comedy of Errors* (c.1589–94) and *Love's Labour's Lost* (c.1588–97), and of his first Roman play, *Titus Andronicus* (before 1594).

He was also working in the early 1590s on his early history plays, *Henry VI* Parts i, ii, and iii (c.1589–93) and *Richard III* (c.1592–94), and by the end of the decade had produced one of his most successful comedies, *A Midsummer Night's Dream* (c.1595–96), along with *The Merchant of Venice* (c.1596) with its mixture of romantic comedy and near-tragedy, and the lovers' tragedy *Romeo and Juliet* (c.1594–96). During this remarkably productive spell – a time when records show that Shakespeare's young son, Hamnet, died and was buried in Stratford – he also produced the series of four dramas which take English history from reign of Richard II in the late Fourteenth Century to the military triumphs of Henry V, *Richard II* (c.1595), *Henry IV* Parts i and ii (c.1598–1600), and *Henry V* (c.1599). The two 'mature comedies', *As You Like It* (c.1598–1600), and *Twelfth Night* (c.1600–02) were probably written towards the end of the decade.

Around the turn of the century, Shakespeares's plays became darker in mood, with the production of the three so-called 'problem' plays, *All's Well That Ends Well* (c.1601–05), *Measure for Measure* (c.1603–04), and *Troilus and Cressida* (c.1601–02), and the four great tragedies, *Hamlet* (c.1599–1601), *Othello* (c.1603–04), *King Lear* (1605–06) and *Macbeth* (c.1606–07). Following the tragedies, he produced his last great plays, the haunting and often mystical tragic-comic romances of *Cymbeline* (c.1608–10), *The Winter's Tale* (c.1609–11), and *The Tempest* (c.1611), in which the declaration of the godlike Prospero that he will 'break my staff ... and, deeper than did ever plummet sound, I'll drown my book' is sometimes taken as Shakespeare's own farewell to his art.

All the plays were written specifically for performance by the groups of players with whom Shakespeare worked, and would have been altered, adapted, and reworked through rehearsals: the authoritative version of most of them is generally taken to be that of the so-called First Folio, gathered together after his death and published for the first time in 1623. The only pieces which he wrote to be published were the narrative poems *Venus and Adonis* (1593), *The Rape of Lucrece* (1594), and *The Phoenix and the Turtle* (1601). In addition, his Sonnets, dedicated to the mysterious 'Mr. W. H.' and bound together with the poem *A Lover's Complaint*, appeared in 1609, although there is no reason to suppose that he was involved in the book's publication.

By the end of his life, Shakespeare was a wealthy and successful man. A sneering attack on him by a rival playwright, Robert Greene, who described him as 'an upstart crow, beautified with our feathers', shows how he was inspiring jealousy in the theatrical world as early as 1592; within a few years, he was not only a member of the Lord Chamberlain's Men, London's leading playing company, but also part owner of the new Globe Theatre, on the south bank of the Thames. The prosperity of the company continued to increase alongside that of Shakespeare himself after the accession of James I, when its name was changed to The King's Men, a significant mark of royal favour. In 1597, Shakespeare's wealth enabled him to buy a large house in Stratford-upon-Avon, and eight years later, he invested in a share of the parish tithes in the town. He is also known to have bought at least one investment property in London.

But the real mark of his success was the tributes paid by his colleagues after his death, and by scholars and literary figures ever since. Ben Jonson, his fellow actor and playwright, said that he was 'not of an age but for all time'; John Heminge and Henry Condell, the two actors who gathered his plays together for the First Folio Edition of 1623, declared that they were acting solely to keep his memory alive. John Dryden, Samuel Johnson, and Samuel Taylor Coleridge are only three of the great poets and critics who have written about his work; and if, as he did, Shakespeare stole many of his stories from earlier sources, later writers have paid similar tribute to his own work. Verdi's opera *Macbeth* and Tom Stoppard's *Rosencrantz and Guildenstern are Dead* are two of many works that have a clear debt to his plays. His influence on world literature has been incalculable; and with new words such as 'domineering' and 'fashionable' and well-known phrases like 'dead as a doornail' and 'pound of flesh' all culled from his plays, he has done more to change the English language of everyday speech than any other single writer.

John Donne (1572–1631)

John Donne, Dean of St Paul's and known as one of the most passionate preachers of his or any other age, grew up as a Catholic, but renounced his Catholicism as a young man. Around the same time he was writing his *Satires* and *Elegies*, although the dates of many of his poems are uncertain. He also sailed on military expeditions against the Spanish with the Earl of Essex and Sir Walter Ralegh, but an unwise marriage dashed any hopes of preferment at Court. Donne's *Holy Sonnets* are believed to have been written later in his life, possibly around the time when he agreed to become a clergyman within the Church of England. Donne's poems, particularly the *Holy Sonnets*, mix intense passion with complex, imaginative, and intellectual imagery that leads him to be considered the most important of the Metaphysical school of poets. He also wrote a number of religious and philosophical essays and treatises. Three volumes of his sermons were published after his death, between 1640 and 1660.

Ben Jonson (1572–1637)

Like many of the Elizabethan poets and dramatists, Ben Jonson was a man of many parts – a formidable classical scholar, and sometime bricklayer, soldier, and actor, who served time in prison for sedition and came close to being hanged after killing a man in a duel. He is best known today for his mordant satires, such as *Volpone* (1605), *The Alchemist* (1610), and *Bartholomew Fair* (1614), and for a large number of epigrams and short lyrics. These include his famous song *Drink to me only*, and also one of the most moving short poems in the language, the 12-line *On my first son*, in which he mourns his son's death. King James I recognised the immense respect and affection in which he was held by awarding him a state pension in 1616. Jonson was a close friend of William Shakespeare, of whom he famously declared after his death that he 'loved the man . . . on this side (of) idolatry'. On his own grave in Westminster is the simple but evocative epitaph, 'O rare Ben Jonson'.

Thomas Dekker (1575–1641)

Thomas Dekker was often mocked in Elizabethan London – notably by Ben Jonson – for the unremitting cheerfulness of his plays, many of which are now lost. Those that survive include *The Shoemaker's Holiday* (1599), which tells the story of the rise of the humble shoemaker Simon Eyre to become Lord Mayor of London, and *Patient Grissil* (1603) about the trials and eventual happy and honourable marriage of a virtuous peasant girl. The latter play includes the well-known lullaby *Golden slumbers kiss your eyes*. Dekker was plagued by poverty throughout his life, and was imprisoned at least twice for debt, including one spell of seven years.

Thomas Heywood (c.1570s–1650)

Little is known of Heywood's life: he may have come from Lincolnshire, was probably a student at Peterhouse College, Cambridge, and was certainly active in the London theatre in the early Seventeenth Century. He claimed to have written more than 200 verse plays, along with a number of pamphlets about contemporary life, but most of the plays are now lost. Of those that remain – mostly domestic dramas of English middle-class life – the blank verse tragedy *A Woman Killed With* Kindness

(1607), about the contrasting fortunes of an adulterous and a virtuous woman, is generally considered to be his masterpiece.

John Fletcher (1579–1625)

John Fletcher collaborated with many of the leading figures of Jacobean drama, most famously William Shakespeare, with whom he is believed to have written *Henry VIII* (before 1613), *The Two Noble Kinsmen* (before 1613), and the lost *Cardenio*, and Sir Francis Beaumont. He also was also sole author of about 16 other comedies and tragedies in verse, including the unsuccessful pastoral tragi-comedy *The Faithful Shepherdess* (before 1610) and the tragedy *Valentinian* (before 1610). Fletcher died of the plague in London.

John Webster (c.1580–c.1630)

John Webster was a prosperous businessman in Jacobean London, combining the careers of coach-maker and playwright, and a member of the socially prestigious Merchant Taylors' Company. Most of his verse dramas were written in collaboration with other playwrights, but his modern reputation rests on two major works, *The White Devil* (1609–1612) and *The Duchess of Malfi* (c.1612), both tragedies based on Italian originals. They combine biting contemporary satire with extreme horror and macabre violence – T.S. Eliot described the playwright as 'much obsessed with death' – but also show Webster's moral seriousness and sense of the futility of earthly ambition.

Robert Herrick (1591–1674)

Robert Herrick was the child of a wealthy London goldsmith and, despite his father's death when he was less than two years old, he lived a privileged and comfortable life as a young man. From Cambridge University, he was ordained as a priest and was appointed to the country parish of Dean Prior in Devon. Living both there and in London, he composed lyrics, songs, and religious verses which focused largely on rural customs and traditional festivals, and on romantic and sentimental addresses to young girls. Since he never married, it is generally assumed that these were largely fictional. Herrick's collection of more than 1,100 secular poems, *Hesperides*, was published in 1648, together with a separate volume of religious verse, *Noble Numbers*. He died in his parish, and was buried in an unmarked grave. Herrick is best known for his insistence that the pleasures of life should be seized wherever possible, best instanced in the famous line, 'Gather ye rosebuds while ye may' from his poem *To the Virgins, to make much of Time*.

George Herbert (1593–1632)

George Herbert, younger son of a prominent and aristocratic Welsh family, was one of the leading religious poets of the early Seventeenth Century. Before he was 18, he is said to have told his mother that he was dedicating his poetic talent to God, and he followed a career in the Church, both at Lincoln Cathedral and in country parishes in Huntingdonshire and Wiltshire. He was a Fellow of Trinity College, Cambridge and Public Orator at the University, and was twice elected Member of Parliament for Montgomery. He was also a dedicated musician, and several of his poems, like *The Elixir* ('Teach me, my god and king') and *Antiphon* ('Let all the world in every corner sing'), have been set to music as hymns. His English poems – he also wrote in Greek and Latin – appeared posthumously in a volume entitled *The Temple* (1633), after he asked a friend either to burn them or publish them if he thought they would 'turn to the advantage of any dejected soul'. Herbert's work is marked by the sustained and ingenious imagery which characterises the Metaphysical school of poetry of the Seventeenth Century.

John Milton (1608–1674)

John Milton's *Paradise Lost* (1667), is unchallenged as the greatest epic poem in English. Milton, who is also known for his sonnets and his lyrical poetry such as *Lycidas* (1638), *L'Allegro (The Happy Man)* (1645) and *Il Penseroso (The Thoughtful Man)* (1645), as well as for his combative prose works, was born in London and educated at St. Paul's School and Christ's College, Cambridge. After leaving university, he stayed at his father's home and began a wide-ranging course of private study aiming to fit himself for a career as a poet.

His first published poem in English, the sonnet *On Shakespeare* (1632), with its famous first line, 'What needs my Shakespeare for his honoured bones?' was published anonymously, as was his masque *Comus* (1637), a pastoral drama which had been performed at Ludlow Castle three years earlier. *Lycidas*, a pastoral elegy on the death of a former fellow-student at Cambridge, appeared the following year.

However, for the next 20 years, Milton produced little poetry, apart from some sonnets and other short poems in Latin, Italian, and English. During this time, he spent two years travelling abroad in Italy and France, and also worked as tutor to his nephews in London. There is also a suggestion that he contemplated writing an epic poem based on the stories of King Arthur. However, events in England forced him to concentrate on political affairs rather than literature. As the disputes between King Charles and the supporters of Parliament flared into open conflict with the outbreak of the First Civil War in 1642, Milton, a devout and dedicated Protestant, began to produce pamphlets in support of the Parliamentary cause and in defence of religious, civil, and personal liberties.

The first of these were a series of five tracts against the rule of bishops within the church – a major point of difference between King and Parliament. Then, following the breakdown of his marriage to the daughter of Royalist parents, he wrote a passionate defence of the idea of divorce, *The Doctrine and Discipline of Divorce* (1643), followed by a pamphlet *On Education* (1644) and his famous *Areopagitica* (1644) on the freedom of the press and the evils of censorship.

He was gradually losing his sight – modern scholars believe he could have been suffering from glaucoma – and he was completely blind by 1651. One of his most famous poems is his sonnet on his blindness, *When I consider how my light is spent* (probably 1652). Other well known short poems from this period include his sonnets on the slaughter of Protestants in Piedmont, *Avenge O Lord thy slaughtered saints* (1655), and on his deceased wife, *Methought I saw my late espousèd saint* (possibly 1658).

After the death of King Charles on the scaffold in 1649, Milton defended the decision to execute him in a pamphlet arguing that there was a right for people to punish tyrants who tried to deny their freedom. He was appointed Latin Secretary to the newly-formed Council of State, a role that meant he was responsible for translating official documents into Latin so that they could be read by foreign governments, and – more importantly – composing papers to explain and defend the policies of the Commonwealth. Milton prepared a series of counter-attacks to criticisms published by Royalist supporters on the continent, and also courageously published a defence of republicanism, *The Ready and Easy Way to Establish a Free Commonwealth* (1660), just weeks before the return of Charles II. As someone who had spoken out publicly in favour of the execution of Charles I, Milton was in danger of execution when the Royalists returned, but although he went into hiding briefly, and was arrested, he escaped with a fine after the intervention of the poet and Member of Parliament Andrew Marvell, who had been his assistant for some of his time as Latin Secretary. It was around this time that he began his work on his greatest work, the 11,000-line *Paradise Lost*, which was published in 10 books (later increased to 12) in 1667. Some of it was written at his house in Chalfont St Giles, Buckinghamshire, after he left London to escape the plague. The poem is written in blank verse, which Milton described as 'English heroic verse without rhyme', and describes the war in heaven that leads to the downfall of Satan, the creation of the world, the establishment of Adam and Eve in the Garden of Eden, and their eventual expulsion after Eve is tempted to eat the apple.

The poem is an epic in the classical manner, focused like Homer's *Iliad* and *Odyssey* on the subjects of war, heroism, and love, but given an explicitly Christian character. Its aim, Milton declares in Book I, is to 'justify the ways of God to men.' It is written throughout in a grand style which Milton specifically compares with that of Homer and Virgil, and employs extended similes, often running over several lines, to evoke the size and scale of Satan, the fallen angels, and the whole conflict between God and his angels on which the poem is built. One criticism that is often made is that Satan, with his courageous defiance and his noble anger, is the most attractive character in the poem.

Paradise Lost did not gain immediate admiration, but the second edition, divided into 12 books rather than 10, and with a brief prose introduction to each one, was published in 1674, shortly before Milton's death. By this time, he had produced two further poems. *Paradise Regained* (1671) is a four-book epic which followed Satan's attempts to tempt first Job and then Christ himself, and his eventual dismissal, which finally offered Man the prospect of salvation. It was published in one volume with *Samson Agonistes*, which sees the Old Testament character of Samson struggling, perhaps like Milton, against the despair of imprisonment and blindness. His final victory in destroying his tormentors with himself by pulling down the building where he is being held establishes him as a true Christian hero.

Despite the quiet reception which *Paradise Lost* received on publication, the poem's reputation gradually grew over the following century, and several more editions of the poem appeared before the end of the century.

Richard Crashaw (c.1613–1649)

Richard Crashaw was the son of a well-known Puritan writer and divine, but became a convert to Catholicism in his thirties, fleeing to Paris and then to Italy, where he died. While he was in exile, his religious poems were published as *Steps to the Temple*, and his secular poems as *Delights of the Muses* (both 1646). Crashaw's poetry, known for its rich, florid language and its extravagant imagery, is at its most passionate in his hymns to various saints, most notably his *Hymn to Saint Teresa*, in which he celebrates the ecstasy of martyrdom.

Richard Lovelace (1618–1658)

Richard Lovelace was one of the so-called Cavalier Poets who supported King Charles I in the English Civil Wars. He fought for the King in Scotland, and was later twice imprisoned by Parliament. Although he was heir to extensive lands in Kent, he lost all his possessions because of his support for the Royalist cause, and died in abject poverty. He wrote two plays which are now lost, and a collection of poetry entitled *Lucasta: Epodes, Odes, Sonnets, Songs, etc* (1649), which includes his famous lyric *To Lucasta, Going to the Wars*. A further book of poems, *Lucasta: Posthume Poems*, (1658) was published by his brother after his death. His poem *To Althea, from Prison* (1642), written while he was imprisoned in Westminster Gatehouse by the parliamentary government, contains the famous lines

> 'Stone walls do not a prison make,
> Nor iron bars a cage.'

Abraham Cowley (1618–1667)

Abraham Cowley was a supporter of King Charles I in the English Civil Wars, serving Queen Henrietta Maria in Paris until returning to England to take up medicine after a short spell in prison. His first poem, the epic romance *Pyramus and Thisbe*, was written when he was 10 years old, and published in an early collection, *Poetical Blossoms* (1633). He also wrote a collection of love poems, *The Mistress* (1647), and a collection, *Poems* (1656), which contains the first of his formal odes, based on the model of the Ancient Greek poet Pindar, along with the *Davideis*, an epic account of the biblical story of David. Among his best-known poems are *Ode, Upon the Blessed Restoration* (1660) and *Upon the Death of Mr William Hervey* (1656), a personal elegy for a close friend. He was the most popular and respected poet of his day, although his reputation was eclipsed after his death by his greater contemporaries, particularly John Milton.

Andrew Marvell (1621–1678)

The Yorkshire-born Andrew Marvell was a supporter of the Parliamentary cause after the English Civil Wars, although he avoided much of the fighting by spending the years 1643–1647 travelling in Europe. He was a close friend of John Milton, and followed him in the post of Latin Secretary to the Council of State. He also wrote several political poems as unofficial Poet Laureate under the Protectorate of Oliver Cromwell, including *An Horatian Ode upon Cromwell's Return from Ireland* (1650) and an elegy *Upon the Death of his Late Highness the Lord Protector* (1658). He served as Member of Parliament for Hull for 19 years, and is often credited with using his influence to protect his friend and mentor Milton from prosecution and possible death after the restoration of Charles II. Marvell's *Miscellaneous Poems* (1681) was published after his death, but was largely ignored for 200 years. Today, he is known not only for his political odes and satires, but especially for the detached and often enigmatic tone of lyrics such as *To his Coy Mistress*, *The Nymph complaining for the death of her faun*, and *The Garden*.

Henry Vaughan (1621–1695)

Henry Vaughan, the son of a Welsh gentleman from Breconshire, worked as a lawyer and later as a doctor in Wales. His first publications, *Poems* (1646) and *Olor Iscanus* (*The Swan of Usk*) (1647) were generally secular, and included love poems and translations from Ovid and other classical authors, but his reputation rests on his later religious poetry, such as *Silex*

Scintillans (*The Flashing Flint*) (1650), a collection in which the poems combine an impassioned, mystical quality with a striking directness of expression. Like William Blake more than a century later, Vaughan was fascinated by the idea of childish innocence. Apart from his poetry, he wrote several devotional prose works. A further volume of poetry, *Thalia Rediviva* (*The Muse of comedy restored*), containing poems by Vaughan and his twin brother Thomas, was published in 1678.

John Bunyan (1628–1688)

John Bunyan, the son of a tinker from Bedford – 'one of the meanest and most despised of all the families of the land,' as he put it – was a dedicated Christian preacher, who served in the Parliamentary army in the English Civil Wars. He was imprisoned for nearly 12 years between 1660 and 1672 for preaching without a licence, and later for a brief spell in 1676. During the first period in prison he completed nine religious prose works, including the autobiographical *Grace Abounding to the Chief of Sinners* (1666) and began his masterpiece, *The Pilgrim's Progress* (published in two parts, 1678–1684), during his second spell in prison. His fame as a poet rests on the poem *To be a Pilgrim* from the second part of *The Pilgrim's Progess*, which was adapted as a popular modern hymn. The modern version, 'He who would valiant be 'gainst all disaster' was written in 1906 by the Anglican cleric Percy Dearmer.

John Dryden (1631–1700)

John Dryden had the flexibility to write *Heroic Stanzas* (1658) to mark the death of Oliver Cromwell and then, two years later, *Astraea Redux* (1660), more than 300 lines of rhymed couplets to celebrate the return of King Charles II. Dryden enjoyed a close relationship with Charles, who appointed him Poet Laureate in 1668, and later with his younger brother, James II. It was only after 20 years, with the fall of James II and the accession to the throne of the Protestant William and Mary, that Dryden, who had converted to Catholicism, finally fell from Royal favour. He was a successful writer of plays both in rhyme and in blank verse for the London stage, including the witty tragi-comedy *Secret Love, or the Maiden Queen* (1667), in which King Charles's mistress, Nell Gwynn, took a leading role, and *Sir Martin Mar-all* (1667), an English version of a

French comedy by Molière. Dryden was also one of the leading literary critics of his age, and the author of public poems such as *Annus Mirabilis* (1667), a triumphant celebration of two English naval victories over the Dutch and of London's survival of the Great Fire of 1666. In 1681, he turned his hand to verse satire, and produced some of the wittiest and most biting satires that had been seen in the language. *Absalom and Achitophel* (1681) was a defence of King Charles against his political critics, the Whig party. Another satire, *Mac Flecknoe* (1682) was an anonymous attack on the Whig playwright Thomas Shadwell. After he lost his place at Court, Dryden turned to translating classical authors such as Homer, Virgil, Horace, Ovid, and Juvenal, as well as works by Chaucer and the Renaissance Italian poet Giovanni Boccaccio. He died in London, and was buried in Westminster Abbey, next to Chaucer.

Thomas Traherne (c.1637–1674)

Thomas Traherne was the son of a shoemaker, but is believed to have been brought up by a wealthy innkeeper following the death of both his parents when he was a young child. He was a passionately devout man, who worked as a parish priest for 10 years before being appointed as a chaplain at the Court of King Charles II. He is generally numbered among the English Metaphysical poets, although his poems reflect the mystical view of religion of a man who claimed to see ghosts and experience visions. He was known almost exclusively as a prose writer until two notebooks containing many of his poems and meditations were found on a London bookstall at the end of the Nineteenth Century. The poems were originally attributed to Henry Vaughan, but were published as Traherne's *Poetical Works* in 1903. A further volume, discovered in the British Museum, was published as *Poems of Felicity* (1910), and other poems believed to be by Traherne have been discovered over the past hundred years.

Aphra Behn (1640–1689)

Aphra Behn was baptised as Aphra Johnson, the daughter of a barber and a domestic servant, in 1640, but lived a shadowy, mysterious, and frequently scandalous life as a traveller, spy, and dramatist. Little is known about her, except that she visited Surinam and returned to London to marry a merchant of Dutch descent named Behn, and worked for Charles II as a spy in Antwerp during the Dutch wars. She then began a career as a playwright with *The Forced Marriage* (1670), which was followed by at least 14 other plays and a number of prose works, including the popular *Oroonoko, of the History of the Royal Slave* (1688). She also established a reputation as a poet during her lifetime, with *Poems Upon Several Occasions, with a Voyage to the Island of Love* (1684), *Miscellany* (1685), and *The Lover in Fashion* (1688). Her work includes formal odes to both Charles II and James II, but the explicit celebrations of free love and sexual passion in her less public poetry led to her acquiring an undeserved reputation as a lewd and licentious writer. Virginia Woolf, naming her as the first English woman to earn her living as a writer, noted that she was buried 'scandalously, but rather appropriately' in Westminster Abbey.

John Wilmot, Earl of Rochester (1647–1680)

Rochester, in Samuel Johnson's famous verdict, 'blazed out his youth and health in lavish voluptuousness'. He was dead at 33, after a death-bed conversion to religion, when he is reputed to have asked that all his 'profane and lewd' writings should be burned. His request was ignored, and so his brilliant lampoons, coruscating satires, and startlingly physical love poetry were saved. One of his more bawdy satires, known from its first line as *In the Isle of Britain*, mocked Charles II's obsession with sex, and led to a brief exile from the King's court. Apart from being a well-known rake and libertine, Rochester was also a Latin scholar who wrote translations of several classical poets, including Ovid, Horace, and Seneca. He had a glittering reputation as a wit who was always ready with impromptu verses, such as his famous summing up of Charles II as a monarch 'who never said a foolish thing, And never did a wise one.'

Thomas Otway (1652–1685)

Thomas Otway was a failed actor – he abandoned his first part after suffering from stage fright – who went on to become a successful playwright. His plays, which won him a glittering contemporary reputation, included the rhyming heroic play *Don Carlos* (1676) and translations from the French writers Racine and Molière. His most famous work, the blank verse tragedy *Venice Preserved* (1682) was frequently performed over the next 300 years. Otway also wrote some non-dramatic verse, including an autobiographical attack on his literary rivals, *The Poet's Complaint of his Muse, or a Satire Against Libels* (1680).

Jonathan Swift (1667–1745)

As the author of *Gulliver's Travels* (1726), *The Tale of a Tub* (1704), and whole series of squibs and pamphlets, including *A Modest Proposal* (1729), in which he suggested that the Irish should defeat poverty by eating their own children, Swift is the leading prose satirist of English literature. He was also a senior figure in the Church, being appointed Dean of St Patrick's Cathedral in Dublin in 1713. Swift's gift for satire was also carried over into poetry, for example in his sharply ironic mock elegy for himself, *Verses on the death of Dr Swift* (1731), in which he imagines the reaction to news of his death. In *On the Death of a Late Famous General* (1726), he was particularly contemptuous of political and military honours. But Swift could also display a more light-hearted attitude in his poems about London, *Description of a City Shower* and *Description of the Morning* (1709), and gentler and more affectionate irony, as in the series of birthday poems he wrote to Stella, the daughter of one of his household servants, whom he met when she was eight years old, and alongside whom he was buried. He is now believed to have suffered for many years from Ménière's disease, a disorder of the inner ear which affects hearing and balance, but the worsening symptoms as he grew older led many people to believe him to be insane.

Matthew Prior (1664–1721)

Matthew Prior was a successful diplomat and occasional secret agent on behalf of the British Government, although shortly after the death of Queen Anne in 1714, he was impeached and imprisoned for two years by the new Whig administration. Among his public poems were an *Ode Presented to the King on his Majesty's Arrival in Holland after The Queen's death* (1695), and a further poem in solemn rhyming couplets marking King William's survival of an assassination attempt the following year, entitled *To the King, at his Arrival in Holland, after the Discovery of the Conspiracy*. The 42 stanzas of his *Carmen Saeculare* (1700) compare King

William to the sun. Such poems brought him considerable wealth and fame, but he is better remembered today for his less serious and self-important occasional verses and epigrams.

William Congreve (1670–1729)

William Congreve studied as a youth to become a lawyer, but the rapid success first of a novel, *Incognita* (1691) and then of his first stage comedy *The Old Bachelor* (1693) encouraged him to become a playwright, with the enthusiastic support of John Dryden. He is considered to be one of the leading figures in Restoration comedy, particularly with *The Double Dealer* (1694), *Love for Love* (1695) and *The Way of the World* (1700). Congreve also wrote formal public poetry and lighter, often wistful love lyrics, such as the brief *False Though She Be* (date uncertain). He is best known, however, for two lines, often misquoted, from his one little-known tragedy, *The Mourning Bride* (1697):

> 'Music hath charms to soothe a savage breast'

and

> 'Heaven has no rage like love to hatred turned,
> Nor hell a fury like a woman scorned.'

Joseph Addison (1672–1719)

Joseph Addison is best remembered today as a prose writer and essayist, who contributed to some of the leading Restoration magazines, such as the *Spectator* and *Tatler*. However, he was also an MP and Government minister, a distinguished Latin scholar, a playwright whose tragedy *Cato* (1713) was a popular success, and the author of a number of popular public poems, most notably *The Campaign* (1705), celebrating the British victory at the Battle of Blenheim.

John Gay (1685–1732)

The only work of John Gay's which is now regularly performed is *The Beggar's Opera* (1728), his burlesque opera set in Newgate Prison. The play, which was produced by a man named John Rich and brought Gay considerable wealth, was said to have made Gay rich and Rich gay. It was followed by a sequel, *Polly* (1729), which was banned from the stage because of its political satire. Gay's other work included plays and librettos, and mock-heroic poetry such as *Rural Sports* (1713) and mock-pastorals such as *The Shepherd's Week* (1714), which were included in his collected *Poems on Several Occasions* (1720). The collection, like *The Beggar's Opera*, was very successful, but Gay was continually plagued by financial anxieties.

Alexander Pope (1688–1744)

Alexander Pope is the acknowledged master of the heroic couplet, the form in which he wrote his greatest poems, including *An Essay on Criticism* (1711), an astonishingly precocious work produced when Pope was only 21, and laying down guidelines for good taste in literature; *The Rape of the Lock* (1714), a brilliant mock-heroic description of a quarrel between two aristocratic families; *The Dunciad*, (1728; final edition 1743), a satire on literary pretension which includes waspish attacks on many of Pope's contemporaries; and the philosophical *Essay on Man* (1734). Pope's reputation sank with the rise of Romanticism in the Nineteenth Century, but today he is generally considered the finest of the Augustan English poets, with a range which included the famous translations of Homer's *Iliad* (1720) and *Odyssey* (1726), elegies, love poetry, and satires. Pope was handicapped during his life by legal discrimination against Catholics and also by his own ill-health – he was severely hunchbacked, and suffered from tuberculosis and a series of debilitating infections. He is one of the most frequently quoted of all English poets, with many of his more memorable lines being treated almost as proverbs, such as 'A little learning is a dangerous thing' and 'To err is human, to forgive, divine'. Such superficial popularity, however, fails to recognise the breadth of his talent, which ranges from the intensely personal passion of *Eloisa to Abelard* (1717) to the philosophical universality of *Essay on Man*.

James Thomson (1700–1748)

James Thomson was born in the Scottish Borders, and turned to writing after abandoning a career as a clergyman. His four-part work in blank verse, *The Seasons* (1726–1730), set the scene for many of the themes of

43

the Romantic poets, and is sometimes thought of as the first nature poem in English. The words for *Rule Britannia* set to music by Thomas Arne, were taken from Thomson's otherwise now-forgotten masque *Alfred* (1740).

Samuel Johnson (1709–1784)

Samuel Johnson's name will always be associated with Boswell's great biography and with his own monumental *Dictionary* (1755), but he was also the author of a prose romance, *Rasselas, Prince of Abyssinia* (1759); an account of his travelling with his biographer, James Boswell, in *A Journey to the Western Isles of Scotland* (1775); a series of biographies named *Lives of the English Poets* (1779–81); the unsuccessful blank verse tragedy *Irene* (1736, performed 1749); and a vast array of journalism, essays, criticism, and accounts of parliamentary speeches. As a poet, his first major achievement was the satire *London* (1738) on the vices and hypocrisies of the city, to be followed by his finest poem, *On the Vanity of Human Wishes* (1749), similarly written in imitation of the Roman poet Juvenal, but ranging much more widely over the spectrum of man's search for power, influence, glory, and learning. Johnson was plagued by ill health and poverty for much of his life, although a Government pension in 1762 relieved him of the pressing necessity to write for a living. He is buried in Westminster Abbey.

Thomas Gray (1716–1771)

Thomas Gray enjoyed great popularity in his time, but today is known almost exclusively for his heavily-anthologised *Elegy in a Country Churchyard* (1751), with its famously evocative line, 'The plowman homeward plods his weary way ...' Among Gray's first English poems – he began his career by writing Latin verse – was his *Ode on a Distant Prospect of Eton College* (1742) which, along with his other early poems, attracted little attention. His Elegy, however, which he wrote at Stoke Poges in Buckinghamshire, while he was a Fellow at Peterhouse College, Cambridge, was an instant success, mourning the graves of the lowly and unknown villagers in language generally reserved for appreciations of the great and powerful. One line from the poem, 'Far from the madding crowd's ignoble strife', was later adopted by the Victorian writer Thomas Hardy as the title for his novel. Gray remained at Peterhouse College, but the unenthusiastic reception to two further poems, *The Progress of Poesy* (1754) and *The Bard* (1757), helped to persuade him to stop writing. He refused the offer of the Poet Laureateship in 1757, and devoted the rest of his life to the study of ancient Celtic and Scandinavian history.

William Collins (1721–1759)

William Collins's career began at the age of 17, when he completed his *Persian Eclogues* (published 1742), in which he transferred traditional English pastoral attitudes to an exotic Middle East setting. The poems, catching the current fashion for the Orient, were well received, and were followed by his *Odes on Several Descriptive and Allegoric Subjects* (1747). Supported by an inheritance, Collins lived the life of a fashionable rake in London, but soon fell into debt, suffered severely from depression, and spent several years in a mental hospital. He was virtually forgotten when he died, but is now considered to have been one of the most influential lyric poets of the Eighteenth Century.

Christopher Smart (1722–1771)

Christopher Smart, a talented classical scholar, suffered from religious mania, and was confined in a private home for the insane in London for several years. His best-known work is his *A Song to David* (1763), a structurally complex poem in which he praises the author of the Psalms and glorifies the Creation and the coming of Christ. Smart was also a productive writer of hymns. Another poem, *Jubilate Agno (Rejoice in the Lamb)* (1758–1763) was written in free verse while the author was in the mental home, and was first published in 1939 after the manuscript was discovered in a private library. Smart died in a debtors' prison in London.

Oliver Goldsmith (1728–1774)

The essayist, novelist, dramatist and poet Oliver Goldsmith, born and educated in Ireland, started his literary career as a reviewer and journalist on various magazines in London. As his reputation as an essayist grew, he became a prominent member of the same circle as Samuel Johnson, and achieved fame with his poem *The Traveller* (1764), which compared conditions in the different countries of Europe, and mourned the decline of the rural life. *The Deserted Village* (1770) continued this theme, as did his famous ironic novel *The Vicar of Wakefield* (1766). Goldsmith then began writing for the theatre, and his verse comedy *She Stoops to Conquer* (1773) was immediately successful. Despite the earnings from his literary successes, Goldsmith fell into severe debt, leading to Samuel Johnson's verdict, 'No man was more foolish when he had not a pen in his hand, or more wise when he had.'

William Cowper (1731–1800)

William Cowper (whose name is correctly pronounced 'Cooper') trained as a lawyer, and took a post for a brief period as an official in the House of Lords, but suffered all his life from mental instability, depression, suicidal tendencies, and fear that he was destined to be damned. He collaborated with a clergyman called John Newton on a volume of hymns, *Olney Hymns* (1779), which include some of Cowper's best-known work, such as *God moves in a mysterious way* and *There is a fountain filled with blood*. In 1785, he published the comic *Diverting History of John Gilpin* and *The Task*, the latter a mock heroic blank verse poem in six books, written in response to a light-hearted request from a friend for a poem about a sofa. His later poetry is known particularly for its simple, direct language, and its concern for the poor and disadvantaged. These qualities, together with a continued interest in country life, make Cowper in many ways a forerunner of the Romantic Movement.

Johann Wolfgang von Goethe (1749–1832)

Johann Wolfgang von Goethe, widely considered to be the most important writer in German literature and one of the leading figures in European culture, is best known for his two-part tragedy *Faust* (1808 and 1832). However, his writings included poetry, philosophy, and science, as well as the Romantic novel *The Sorrows of Young Werther* (1774). Apart from his literary career, he occupied senior positions in the government of Weimar, and established a reputation as an important scientist. His important collections of poetry include *Römische Elegien* (*Roman Elegies*) (1790), *Hermann und Dorothea* (*Hermann and Dorothea*) (1797), and *Der West-östliche Divan* (*The West-East Council of State*) (1819), based on the Persian poetry of Shams ud-din Shafiz. Many of Goethe's lyrical poems were set to music.

Thomas Chatterton (1752–1770)

Thomas Chatterton, the darling of the English Romantic poets, was a precocious genius who died before his eighteenth birthday. Wordsworth referred to him as the 'marvellous boy' and Keats dedicated his poem *Endymion* to his memory. Chatterton was apprenticed to a Bristol lawyer at the age of 15, but dedicated himself to his writing, which he had begun at the age of 10 with an astonishingly mature short poem in the style of Milton entitled *On the Last Epiphany* (1762). He wrote a series of poems purporting to be the work of a fictitious Fifteenth Century Bristol monk named Thomas Rowley, and in 1770 left his employer in Bristol and moved to London, aiming to make a living by writing satires and pamphlets. There, he composed a comic opera *The Revenge*, a satire entitled *Kew Gardens*, and a final poem by 'Rowley', *An Excelente Balade of Charitie*. After a few months, despairing of success and ravaged by poverty, he killed himself with arsenic. Disputes about the authenticity of the Thomas Rowley poems continued for nearly a century before the young Chatterton was finally accepted as their author.

George Crabbe (1754–1832)

George Crabbe's most famous poem *The Village* (1783) was written in response to the idyllic descriptions of rural life that were common in Eighteenth Century poetry, most particularly in Oliver Goldsmith's *The Deserted Village*. Crabbe combined the elevated heroic couplets of the Augustan poets with a grim picture of the poverty and hardship which were the reality for many country families. He published nothing for 22 years, and then produced a series of narrative verses, *The Borough* (1810), *Tales in Verse* (1812), and *Tales of the Hall* (1819). The Twentieth Century composer, Benjamin Britten based his opera *Peter Grimes* on verses from *The Borough*.

William Blake (1757–1827)

At his death, William Blake was considered to be insane even by those who admired his work as a poet, artist, and engraver; today, he is known for the delicate but forceful lyrics such as 'Little lamb, who made thee?' from *Songs of Innocence* (1789) and 'Tyger, tyger, burning bright' from

Songs of Experience (1794), and for the hymn known as *Jerusalem* (c.1804), set to music by Sir Hubert Parry in 1916. Confusingly, Blake wrote another poem named *Jerusalem (1804–1820)*; the hymn is an introductory lyric to his long poem *Milton* (1804–1808). A professional engraver and a talented water colourist, he etched, printed, and illustrated his poems and sold them himself, a few at a time. Blake was a mystic and visionary Christian who developed his political philosophy of revolt against authority combined with a highly idiosyncratic version of Christianity though works such as *The Marriage of Heaven and Hell* (1790–1793) and the deeply symbolic *The Four Zoas* (1795–1804). His ideas led to an unsuccessful prosecution for treason in 1893, and his poems were virtually unnoticed until nearly 40 years after his death. Today, Blake is recognised as an original and unique talent, and widely seen as a precursor to the Romantic poets.

Robert Burns (1759–1796)

Robert Burns, whose iconic *Auld Lang Syne* (1788) marks the traditional Hogmanay or New Year's Eve, is unchallenged as Scotland's national poet. Much of his poetry is written in a restrained version of the Scottish dialect of English, although he also wrote in Scots and in Standard English. He was originally a small tenant farmer in Scotland, but despite his passionate radical politics, he later became a Government Excise officer. From his youth, he wrote romantic songs and ballads, and published his first collection, *Poems, Chiefly in the Scottish Dialect* in 1786. The book, which included such favourite lines as 'Wee sleekit, cow'rin, tim'rous beastie' (*To a Mouse*), was an immediate success, and Burns became a national hero virtually overnight. With another poem in the book, *Address to the De'il*, he established himself as a rebel against accepted religious thinking, while his later song *a Man's a Man For A' That* (1795) reflects his lifelong egalitarianism. Burns maintained a lifelong interest in traditional Scottish music and folksongs, but poems such as *Tam O'Shanter* (1791) show that he was also a dedicated and innovative stylist and craftsman in his own right. His satires and verse letters are often considered to be his best work, but it is the popular songs that are remembered most forcefully, particularly on Burns Night, which is celebrated around the world on his birthday, January 25.

James Hogg (1770–1835)

James Hogg, a poor shepherd from Ettrick Forest in the Scottish Borders, was encouraged by Sir Walter Scott and lionised by the poets of the Romantic Movement as the Ettrick Shepherd. He published *The Mountain Bard*, a collection of ballads, in 1807, and a further collection of poems about Mary, Queen of Scots, *The Queen's Wake* in 1813. He also wrote several novels, one of which, *Confessions of a Justified Sinner* (1824) is now considered his most important work.

William Wordsworth (1770–1850)

William Wordsworth was probably the most important figure in the birth of the English Romantic movement in poetry. He was the author, along with Samuel Taylor Coleridge, of the *Lyrical Ballads* (1798) which provided a practical manifesto for a new way for poets to look at the world – and yet, by the end of his long life, he was rejected and reviled by many of the great figures who had followed in his footsteps.

The difference between his early and late work was famously summarised by the poet and humorist J.K. Stephen, who wrote: 'Two voices are there: one is of the deep ... And one is of an old half-witted sheep, Which bleats articulate monotony.'

Wordsworth was born in Cockermouth, on the fringes of the Lake District of northern England. His mother died when he was seven and his father six years after, and he was sent away to school at Hawkshead in the rural heart of the Lake District. There 'fostered alike by beauty and by fear,' as he described later in his autobiographical poem *The Prelude* (published 1850) he was first fired by his enthusiasm for nature.

Cambridge University did not greatly interest him, and he left with an unimpressive 'pass' degree – but while he was there he set off on a walking tour in 1790 to France, then in the early days of the French Revolution. His early enthusiasm for nature was matched by his passionate support for revolutionary ideas, and he returned to France the following year. A woman he met there, Annette Vallon, bore him a daughter – but not until after he had left for home. Separated from them by the wars between England and France, he never saw mother or child until his daughter Caroline was 10 years old, when he travelled to France to visit them shortly before his marriage in 1802. His sonnet *It is a beauteous evening, calm and free* (1802) movingly records an evening walk with Caroline on the beach.

In 1797, along with his sister Dorothy, he had moved to Bristol, soon after meeting Coleridge for the first time. Wordsworth had been struggling unsuccessfully to write long narrative and descriptive poems, but, along with Coleridge, he now turned his attention to short lyrical and dramatic poems focused on nature and ordinary daily life. Many of them, including Coleridge's *The Rime of the Ancient Mariner* and Wordsworth's *Tintern Abbey*, were gathered together in the first edition of *Lyrical Ballads* (1798). It was followed by further, expanded editions in 1800 and 1802, in which the poets set out their determination to write honestly and directly about true feeling, rather than with the 'gaudiness and inane phraseology' of Eighteenth Century writing. Poetry, said the book's introduction, 'takes its origin from emotion recollected in tranquillity'. Among the poems added to these later editions were the so-called 'Lucy' lyrics, such as the famous *She dwelt among the untrodden ways*.

Many of the poems were initially ridiculed by critics for the simplicity of their diction and the homeliness of their subject matter – but the literary revolution had started.

Wordsworth moved with Dorothy back to the Lake District, where in 1802 he married a friend from his childhood, Mary Hutchinson. He had already started work on the long autobiographical poem that would stay with him for the next 40 years, *The Prelude, or Growth of a Poet's Mind*. He claimed later that it was finished in 1805, but he kept revising it for the rest of his life, and it was not published until after his death.

He took up a government post as distributor of stamps for the county of Westmorland, and continued to write poetry, with the death at sea of his brother John inspiring him to write several poems, including *Elegiac Stanzas Inspired by a Picture of Peele Castle* (1807). Among the books he produced during this period of middle-age were *Poems in Two Volumes* (1807), which included the famous *Sonnet Composed upon Westminster Bridge* and the lyric *Daffodils*, with perhaps the best-known opening line in English literature, 'I wandered lonely as a cloud'; *The Excursion* (1814), which was part of a projected longer poem which was never finished, *The Recluse*, which included laments for the deaths of two of his children; and his *Collected Poems* (1815). He had by this time been estranged from Coleridge for several years, partly because of the latter's addiction to opium and partly because of what Coleridge saw as Wordsworth's abandonment of his earlier revolutionary principles.

He was still suffering repeated attacks from critics and reviewers. However, although modern critics generally agree that Wordsworth's creative period ended with the publication of the 1815 collection, the relatively bland descriptive poems that he wrote later in his life, inspired by his travels in Europe, Scotland, and along the River Duddon in Cumbria, were popular in his day, and helped to build his reputation as a deep and sensitive thinker. Byron, Shelley, and Keats, who had never retracted their bitter criticisms of Wordsworth as 'simple' and 'dull', were all dead by 1824, and though Robert Browning later derided him in his poem *The Lost Leader* (1845) as a radical who had abandoned his principles 'just for a handful of silver', their voices did nothing to lessen his public esteem. He was awarded an annual Civil List pension in 1842, and named Poet Laureate the following year. He died at the home he had lived in since 1813, Rydal Mount, near Ambleside, Cumbria, shortly after completing revisions for a final authoritative six-volume edition of his poems (1849–50).

Today, he is valued particularly for the shorter lyrics of his earlier years, and for his role as the first and possibly the greatest of the Romantic poets. Wordsworth's *Preface* to the second edition of *Lyrical Ballads* set out the manifesto for the Romantic movement, and his own poetry – most notably *The Prelude*, the first long autobiographical poem in English – brought it to fruition.

Sir Walter Scott (1771–1832)

Sir Walter Scott's first big success, *The Lay of the Last Minstrel* (1805) was a long narrative poem in six cantos, set in the Sixteenth Century and based on an old legend of the Scottish Borders. Scott had started on a legal career, but had developed a passionate interest in traditional ballads that led to several more poetic romances, including *Marmion* (1808), which includes the frequently quoted lines:

> 'Oh what a tangled web we weave
> When first we practise to deceive.'

Other successful titles were *The Lady of the Lake* (1810), *Rokeby* (1813) and *Lord of the Isles* (1815). Scott also edited editions of the poetry of John

Dryden and Jonathan Swift, but from 1814 on he concentrated on writing his hugely successful historical novels. These appeared anonymously, starting with *Waverley* (1814) and including *Rob Roy* (1817), *The Heart of Midlothian* (1818), and *Ivanhoe* (1819). Their popularity led to his baronetcy in 1820, but despite the fortune which they made for him, Scott suffered from financial problems for most of his life, striving to pay off his creditors until his death.

Samuel Taylor Coleridge (1772–1834)

Samuel Taylor Coleridge, the son of a respectable West Country clergyman, is known as the co-founder, along with his friend and fellow political radical William Wordsworth, of the English Romantic movement with the publication of their joint collection, *Lyrical Ballads* (1798). This included the first version of his famous ballad *The Rime of the Ancient Mariner*. Among his other best-known poems are *Frost at Midnight* (1798), *Dejection, an Ode* (1802), and *Kubla Khan* (1816), which was originally composed in 1797, but is famously unfinished because Coleridge's opium-induced dream was interrupted by a visitor. His great prose work, *Biographia Literaria* (1817) mixes autobiography, philosophy, and literary criticism. The last 20 years of Coleridge's life were marred by political disillusionment, increasing addiction to opium, the breakup of his marriage, and a lasting rift with his friend Wordsworth.

Robert Southey (1774–1843)

Robert Southey, one of the Romantic Lake Poets, and close friend and brother-in-law of S.T. Coleridge, was appointed Poet Laureate in 1813. By then, he was already the respected author of two plays and several lyrics, ballads and narrative poems, including *The Inchcape Rock* (1820), *Madoc* (1805), and *The Curse of Kehama* (1810). He was also involved in a public, lasting, and bitter feud with Lord Byron, over his retreat from political radicalism and acceptance of many Tory ideas. Southey is also known as an essayist and master of prose style, with biographies including the *Life of Nelson* (1813) and histories such as his *History of the Peninsular War* (1823–32) and *History of Brazil* (1810–19) to his credit. His final years were overshadowed by the insanity of his wife and his own increasing mental problems.

Walter Savage Landor (1775–1864)

Walter Savage Landor was a great favourite of the Victorians, particularly Robert Browning, but is little remembered today. His most famous work was the prose *Imaginary Conversations of Literary Men and Statesmen* (1824–29) but he also wrote a seven-book epic poem, *Gebir* (1798) and a verse drama, *Count Julian* (1812). He was more successful in his brief epigrams, but even here, the emotion is often weighed down by a ponderous self-importance.

Charles Lamb (1775–1834)

Charles Lamb devoted most of his life to the care of his sister Mary, after she murdered their mother in a fit of insanity. With her he wrote the famous *Tales from Shakespeare* (1807), and he developed a considerable reputation as an essayist and critic in his own right with *Essays of Elia* (1823) and other collections. Lamb contributed poems to several anthologies published during his life, most notably *The Old Familiar Faces* (1798), a regretful meditation on lost friends and relationships, and the subtle and delicate elegy *On an Infant Dying as Soon as Born* (1827).

Thomas Moore (1779–1852)

The Irish satirist and poet Thomas Moore was a close friend of Lord Byron, and the author of the hugely popular *Lalla Rookh* (1817) a series of lush and extravagant oriental verse tales. Before that, he had published *Epistles, Odes, and Other Poems* (1806) and started work on a series of poems eventually published as *Irish Melodies* (1801–34), which included several famous songs such as *The Minstrel Boy* and *The Last Rose of Summer*. His *Twopenny Post Bag* (1813) was a collection of satires aimed at the Prince Regent. He was also responsible, along with the publisher John Murray, for burning Byron's memoirs after his death.

Leigh Hunt (1784–1859)

Leigh Hunt, the son of a poor London clergyman, is best known as an essayist and critic, who was an early supporter of John Keats and the Romantic Movement. His own poem, *The Story of Rimini* (1816), reputedly written with the help of Lord Byron, tells Dante's story of the love and death of Paolo and Francesca. *Jenny Kissed Me*, a light-hearted but defiant poem about memory, youth and age, is believed to have been written around 1835. Among Hunt's other publications were the collections *Foliage* (1818) and *The Book of Gems* (1838), which contained his well-known poem *Abou Ben Adhem*.

Thomas Love Peacock (1785–1866)

Thomas Love Peacock was the son of a prosperous London glass merchant, and spent most of his life as an administrator at the East India Company. He had published two books of verse, *The Monks of St Mark* (1804) and *Palmyra and Other Poems* (1805) and a poem, *The Genius of the Thames* (1810), based on a journey on foot down the river, before meeting Percy Bysshe Shelley in 1812. Under Shelley's influence, he started work on *Headlong Hall* (1816) and the other comic-satirical novels, incorporating songs and verses, which were to prove his most lasting achievement.

George Gordon, Lord Byron (1788–1824)

Byron's early childhood was spent in relative poverty in Aberdeen until, just 10 years old, he unexpectedly inherited the title and wealth of his great-uncle, the Fifth Baron Byron, known as the Wicked Lord. He led a dissipated life at Cambridge University and his first collection of poems, *Hours of Idleness* (1807), was savaged by a reviewer and made little impact. However, while travelling in Europe he wrote the first two cantos of his long poem *Childe Harold's Pilgrimage* (1812), which was wildly popular. This was followed by several other famous poems, including *The Giaour* (1813), *The Bride of Abydos* (1813), and *Lara* (1814). However, dogged by financial troubles and rumours of incest with his half-sister, Augusta Leigh, Byron left to travel in Europe again, writing two further cantos of *Childe Harold's Pilgrimage* and a mock heroic poem, *Beppo* (1817). He also started work on his most famous poem *Don Juan* (1819–1824), a brilliantly satirical and comic picaresque verse tale, which was unfinished at his death. Byron, a lifelong and outspoken political radical, threw his influence behind Greek resistance to Turkish occupation, but died of fever at Missolonghi before he saw any serious military action.

Percy Bysshe Shelley (1792–1822)

Percy Bysshe Shelley was born into a life of privilege and prosperity, but from the day that his first major poem, *Queen Mab* (1813) appeared, printed by himself and distributed to friends, he shocked Nineteenth Century England with his revolutionary political idealism. Two years after *Queen Mab*, Shelley wrote *Alastor, or the Spirit of Solitude* (1816), which was followed by the *Hymn to Intellectual Beauty* (1817) – written while Shelley was staying with his friend Byron in Switzerland – the bitter political satire *The Mask of Anarchy* (1819), *Prometheus Unbound* (1820), and *Adonais* (1821), an elegy inspired by the death of John Keats. The following year, still only 29, he was drowned in a storm while sailing off the Italian coast near Livorno. On the strength of short poems such as *Ozymandias* (1818), *Ode to the West Wind* (1820) and *To a Skylark* (1820), Shelley is considered one of English Literature's finest lyric poets.

John Clare (1793–1864)

John Clare was a Northamptonshire farm labourer who became one of the most admired minor figures of the English Romantic Movement. His first book, *Poems Descriptive of Rural Life and Society* (1820) caught the contemporary fascination with the countryside and peasant life, and was a significant success. Three further books, *The Village Minstrel* (1821), *The Shepherd's Calendar* (1827), and *The Rural Muse* (1835) followed, but failed to achieve similar popularity. Clare was constantly troubled by mental problems, and was admitted to an asylum in 1837. He wrote more poetry from the asylum, such as *I am, yet what I am who cares or knows* (published 1865). Earlier poems such *Remembrances* and *The Flitting* link a personal wistful nostalgia to a sense of regret for the passing of the traditional rural life with the advance of the Industrial Revolution.

John Keats (1795–1821)

John Keats, the son of a livery stable manager in the City of London, was an orphan by the age of 14. His father died in an accident when the boy was eight, and his mother of tuberculosis six years later, leaving Keats with two younger brothers and a younger sister, to whom he remained deeply attached throughout his life.

He was sent to school in Enfield, about two miles away, and then apprenticed to a surgeon at the age of 16. Three years later, he abandoned his apprenticeship to go and study at Guy's and St. Thomas' Hospitals in London. He was licensed as an apothecary in 1816, but he had begun writing poetry – one of his first works, *Imitation of Spenser*, was written while he was an apprentice – and with the publication of his first collection, *Poems* (1817), he decided to devote his life to writing, not medicine.

This first volume of poetry, including *I stood tip-toe upon a little hill* and *Sleep and Poetry*, attracted a few favourable reviews, but failed to sell many copies. A few months after publication came the start of a series of bitter attacks on Keats's poetry by the influential John Gibson Lockhart in *Blackwood's Magazine*. Even though Keats had also had his sonnets *On first looking into Chapman's Homer* and *O Solitude* published in the prestigious *Examiner* magazine, Lockhart's attacks continued to dog him, and his decision to concentrate on poetry left him in financial difficulties for the rest of his life.

He had already started work on *Endymion*, his retelling of the Greek legend of the love between the moon goddess Diana and the mortal shepherd Endymion, and the poem, some four thousand lines of rhyming couplets arranged in four books, was published in 1818. It describes Endymion's attempt to transform an imagined and idealistic love into reality and achieve a mystical union with the whole of creation. Today, its theme and its opening line, 'A thing of beauty is a joy for ever' are seen as among the most poignant expressions of the Romantic vision, but the poem sparked another bitter attack from Lockhart, who described it as 'drivelling idiocy'. Keats responded to these criticisms with outward defiance, declaring in a letter 'I think I shall be among the English poets after my death'. *Endymion*, he admitted, showed inexperience and immaturity, but he was intent on 'fitting myself for verses fit to live.'

Later in the year, however, he had greater difficulties to contend with. His brother Tom, with whom he was living in Hampstead, had been suffering from tuberculosis, and Keats looked after him as he sickened and died during the autumn. Shortly afterwards, ominously, he began to suffer from sore throats and coughing fits similar to those which had affected his brother in the early stages of his illness.

About the same time as his brother's final illness, Keats met Fanny Brawne, who soon afterwards became his neighbour in Hampstead with her mother. Keats was immediately struck by her, and fell passionately in love. Over the next 12 months – a period beginning in the autumn of 1818 – most of Keats's greatest poetry was written, to be published in *Lamia, Isabella, The Eve of St Agnes, and Other Poems* (1820). Apart from the title poems, this second collection included his odes *On a Grecian Urn, To a Nightingale, On Melancholy,* and *To Autumn,* and also *Hyperion, Fancy,* and a number of other poems. *The Eve of St Agnes* was published separately a couple of months earlier.

Lamia, Isabella, The Eve of St Agnes, and Other Poems contained an apology from Keats for the unfinished state of *Hyperion,* which describes the plotting of the fallen Titans to regain power over the Olympian Gods. He had planned, he said, to write another four-thousand-line Romantic epic, but had been discouraged by the critical reception given to *Endymion.* He continued to work at the poem, and a later version, *The Fall of Hyperion* (1856) was published 35 years after his death.

Another famous poem, his sonnet *Bright star, would I were steadfast as thou art,* is believed to have been written about this time, and inscribed in a friend's copy of Shakespeare's poems, but was not published until 1838.

Keats's odes, in particular, with their lush, sensuous descriptions, their rich imagery, and their intense philosophical meditations on the contrast between the transience of earthly, physical things and the poet's yearning for constancy and eternity, represent one of the most astonishing collections of lyric verse in English literature. The collection as a whole won considerable critical acclaim, with even *Blackwood's Magazine* expressing a degree of appreciation, but again, the book failed to sell well in Keats's lifetime.

By the time it appeared, in July of 1820, Keats's tuberculosis was in its terminal phase. He was nursed in Hampstead for several months by a group of friends, including Fanny Brawne and her mother, but by September 1820 it was clear that he was dying, and he was ordered south for the winter, leaving Fanny behind in London. He died the following February in Rome at the age of 25, and was buried there with an epitaph that he had written for himself: 'Here lies one whose name was writ in water.'

This final expression of disappointment with his achievement, coming just a few months after he wrote to his friend Shelley that his mind 'was like a pack of scattered cards', was belied by the steady growth in his reputation in the years after his death. Shelley – who had offered him the use of his own residence in Pisa, and who died the following year with a copy of Keats's poetry in his pocket – wrote his famous elegy, *Adonais* in his honour. The publication of collections of his letters in 1848 and 1878 revealed the profundity of his thoughts on poetry, as well as the strengths of his passions about love, beauty, and human relationships.

Keats's standing continued to grow during the Twentieth Century, and he is now seen not simply as a major figure in the Romantic movement, but also as perhaps the greatest lyric poet in the English language.

Hartley Coleridge (1796–1849)

Hartley Coleridge, the son of S.T. Coleridge, showed early promise, but forfeited a fellowship at Oriel College, Oxford, because of his drinking and wild living. He contributed to London magazines, and worked as a schoolmaster at various schools in the north of England. His *Poems, Songs and Sonnets* (1833) attracted little attention, although some of the sonnets and short lyrics are still read. Hartley Coleridge's main claim to literary fame is as the subject of his father's poem, *Frost at Midnight* (1798), which is addressed to the two-year-old boy as he lies sleeping.

Thomas Hood (1799–1845)

Thomas Hood was a successful London journalist, the editor of a number of magazines. He wrote many short, humorous poems and occasional verses, often involving clever puns – Holland, he said, was so low-lying that its people were only saved by being dammed. His sombre and wistful poem *I Remember, I Remember* was included in *The Plea of the Mid-Summer Fairies* (1827). But Hood also had serious social concerns, reflected in *The Song of the Shirt* (1843), in which he highlighted the plight of low-paid workers, and *The Bridge of Sighs* (1844), about the suicide of a 'fallen woman' cast out by society.

Thomas Babington Macaulay, Lord Macaulay (1800–1859)

Thomas Babington Macaulay was the son of a senior public servant and well-known abolitionist, and followed his father into public life as a Member of Parliament and Government Minister. He wrote a popular four-volume *History of England* (1849–55), which led to his elevation to the peerage in 1857. His great poetic work, the *Lays of Ancient Rome* (1842), was a collection of stirring and simple ballads about Roman history, including the story of how Horatius 'kept the bridge in the brave days of old'.

Thomas Lovell Beddoes (1803–1849)

Thomas Lovell Beddoes began the work for which he is best known, *Death's Jest Book, or the Fool's Tragedy*, as a 22-year-old medical student, and continued to revise and work on it throughout his life. It is a blank verse play, heavily influenced by the Jacobean dramatists, and focused on death, decay, and dissolution. It was still unfinished when he died, and was first published in 1850, a year after his death. It has hardly ever been staged, but lyrics from it – particularly the mournful *Wolfram's Dirge*, which offers death as the only cure for the pain of love – are occasionally found in anthologies. Beddoes lived mainly in Germany and Switzerland, and committed suicide in 1849.

Edward Bulwer-Lytton, First Baron Lytton (1803–1873)

Edward Bulwer-Lytton was an active politician and an early supporter of political reform, although he later became a government minister under the Tories. His fame and reputation rest largely on his success as a popular novelist, as the author of more than 20 novels, including *Eugene Aram* (1832) and *The Last Days of Pompeii* (1834). His first published book, however, was *Ismael and Other Poems* (1820), and although this was not a success, he continued writing narrative poems throughout his life, publishing a volume of *Collected Poems* (1831), and translations of Horace and the German poet Friedrich von Schiller. Bulwer-Lytton, who was raised to the peerage in 1866, was also famous for his stormy marriage with the Irish beauty Rosina Doyle Wheeler, which lasted barely five years but led to lasting, bitter, and very public recriminations.

Elizabeth Barrett Browning (1806–1861)

After secretly marrying and eloping together in 1846 to escape her tyrannical father, Elizabeth Barrett Browning and the poet Robert Browning went to Italy, where they stayed for the rest of her life. *The Seraphim, and Other Poems* (1838) was an initial success, followed by *Poems* (1844). Her most famous works were *Sonnets from the Portuguese* (1850), a collection of poems following the progress of her love for Browning (*The Portuguese* refers to Browning's nickname for her) and *Aurora Leigh* (1857), an 11,000-line 'novel in verse' about the life and passionate love affair of a woman poet. During her lifetime, she was thought of as a better poet than her husband, and considered as a possible successor to William Wordsworth as Poet Laureate, although the outspoken radical political ideas of her final book, *Poems Before Congress* (1860) troubled some readers. Her death – in Italy, in her husband's arms – ended one of the iconic love stories of the Nineteenth Century.

Henry Wadsworth Longfellow (1807–1882)

Henry Wadsworth Longfellow, one of the leading American poets of the Nineteenth Century, was a professor of modern languages at Harvard who travelled extensively through Europe. His collection of poems, *Voices of the Night* (1839) brought him fame, and was followed by *Ballads and Other Poems* (1841), which was a runaway success. Long narrative poems such as *Evangeline* (1847), the story of two American lovers separated by British forces, *The Song of Hiawatha* (1855) and *The Courtship of Miles Standish* (1858) were also enthusiastically received. Longfellow produced a classic translation of Dante Alighieri's *Divine Comedy* and six memorable sonnets about the poet and his 'thoughtful pace and sad, majestic eyes'. He also wrote an American series, *Tales of a Wayside Inn* (first series 1863), modelled on Chaucer's *Canterbury Tales*, the first poem of which, *Paul Revere's Ride*, became an American classic. Longfellow's later years were blighted by the death of his wife in an accident at home.

John Greenleaf Whittier (1807–1892)

The Quaker poet John Greenleaf Whittier, born in Haverhill, Massachusetts, was a committed Abolitionist, who wrote impassioned anti-slavery poems in his collection *Voices of Freedom* (1846). His first book of poems, *Legends of New England* (1831) had failed to achieve significant success, and he threw himself wholeheartedly as legislator, journalist and pamphleteer into the campaign against slavery. However, he continued to write poetry, and produced several books of verse, among them *Songs of Labor* (1850), *The Panorama* (1846), and *Home Ballads and Poems* (1860). Among his best-known poems are *Snow-bound* (1866), a nostalgic evocation of long winter evenings spent with his family, and *Barbara Frietchie* (1864), a tale of the Civil War which includes the famous lines ' "Shoot if you must this old grey head, But spare your country's flag," she said.' Further long narrative poems in a similarly mellow, contemplative vein followed, including *The Tent on the Beach* (1867), *Among the Hills* (1868), and *The Pennsylvania Pilgrim* (1872), and Whittier was lionised in his old age as one of the grand old men of American literature.

Edgar Allan Poe (1809–1849)

Edgar Alan Poe is best known for his macabre tales of horror and mystery, particularly *The Fall of the House of Usher*, which was included in his collection *Tales of the Grotesque and Arabesque* (1839), and his early detective story *The Murders in the Rue Morgue* (1841). Before he began writing short stories, however, he had published three volumes of poetry, the last of which, *Poems* (1831) contained the famous *To Helen*, about his memories of a beautiful woman he had known in his childhood. A later revision of this poem (1845) contains the famous lines 'the glory that was Greece, And the grandeur that was Rome'. His poem *The Raven* (1845), with its description of the 'fantastic terrors' of the mysterious bird, was a huge success, but Poe struggled with sickness and alcoholism until his death.

Edward Fitzgerald (1809–1883)

Edward Fitzgerald's great work, *The Rubáiyát of Omar Khayyam* (1859), with its stirring and memorable opening 'Awake! For morning in the bowl of night Hath flung the stone that puts the stars to flight' is a very free translation and interpretation of the work of the Twelfth Century Persian poet. *Rubáiyát* is a Persian word meaning 'quatrains'. Four different versions were published during his lifetime, and a fifth in 1889, six years after his death. Fitzgerald, a Persian scholar and close friend of several leading literary figures including Alfred, Lord Tennyson, lived as a prosperous country gentleman on his family's estate in Suffolk.

Alfred Tennyson, Lord Tennyson (1809–1892)

Alfred Tennyson began writing poetry as a boy, and published his first book, confusingly entitled *Poems by Two Brothers* (1826), in collaboration with two of his brothers at the age of 17. His first adult collection, *Poems, Chiefly Lyrical* (1830) was unenthusiastically reviewed, but a second collection followed two years later, including such favourites as *The Lotus Eaters* and *The Lady of Shallot*. The death of his close friend Arthur Hallam in 1833 – to be marked by the publication 18 years later of Tennyson's finest work, the 132-stanza elegy *In Memoriam* (1850) – seems to have inspired an outpouring of poetry, including *Ulysses* and *The Two Voices*. A new two-volume collection in 1842 contained some earlier poems as well as previously unseen work such as *Morte d'Arthur*, on which Tennyson had been working for several years, and *Locksley Hall*. Appointed Poet Laureate in 1850, he was the best-loved poet of his age, and *Maud and Other Poems* (1855) and *Idylls of the King* (1856–1885) confirmed this popularity. Some of Tennyson's public poetry, like *The Charge of the Light Brigade* (1854) may seem over-simple and even jingoistic today, but he is widely seen as one of the greatest and most influential lyric poets of the later Nineteenth Century. Tennyson was made a peer in 1884, and is buried in Westminster Abbey.

Edward Lear (1812–1888)

Edward Lear was the twentieth child of a failed London stockbroker. He earned his living as a draughtsman, illustrator, and artist, specialising at first in pictures of birds and then establishing himself as a landscape painter, travelling through Europe, the Middle East, and India. After working on a commission to draw animals from the Earl of Derby's private menagerie, he produced *A Book of Nonsense* (1845) for the Earl's grandchildren. Later nonsense volumes were *Nonsense Songs, Stories, Botany and Alphabets* (1871), which contained *The Owl and the Pussy-Cat*; *More Nonsense* (1872); and *Laughable Lyrics* (1877). Lear, who suffered from epilepsy and severe depression throughout his life, also published several volumes of bird and animal drawings and many illustrated travel books.

Robert Browning (1812–1889)

The young Robert Browning, the son of a Bank of England clerk, received little formal education, but a lifetime of private reading, which started in his father's extensive private library, enabled him to become the most famous writer of imaginative and historical dramatic monologues in English. His poem *Paracelsus* (1835) was well received, but his elopement with the poet Elizabeth Barrett, who became his wife in Italy, scandalised much of Victorian London. Browning's collection *Dramatic Lyrics* (1842), including the iconic *My Last Duchess*, failed to win much popularity, as did *Men and Women* (1855). However, when he returned to England after his wife's death in 1861, the 22 poems in *Dramatis Personae* (1864) established him as a popular poet, and his great work, the 21,000-line *The Ring and the Book* (1868–1869), telling the story of a Seventeenth Century murder trial in Rome, easily outsold all his earlier books.

Emily Brontë (1818–1848)

Emily Brontë is best known as the author of the novel *Wuthering Heights* (1847), but her first published work appears in a book written jointly with her two sisters, Charlotte and Anne, *Poems by Currer, Ellis, and Acton Bell* (1846). The male pseudonyms were chosen because of contemporary prejudice against woman writers. The book sold only two copies during Emily Brontë's lifetime, but some of her 21 poems, notably *The Prisoner* and *Remembrance*, are still regarded as classics of the romantic genre. Her poem *Last Lines* ('No coward soul is mine . . .') is also frequently quoted.

Charles Kingsley (1819–1875)

Charles Kingsley was a Victorian clergyman and social campaigner whose novels, aimed at both children and adults, achieved great popularity. They ranged from *Alton Locke* (1850), which tells a story of its hero's struggle against harsh working conditions, to the historical novel *Hereward the Wake* (1866) and the children's fantasy story *The Water Babies* (1863). Kingsley, who became chaplain to Queen Victoria and a professor of history at Cambridge University, also wrote several well-known songs and ballads, including *The Sands of Dee* and *Airly Beacon*.

Arthur Hugh Clough (1819–1861)

Arthur Hugh Clough was an academic, teacher, and examiner who struggled with religious doubt throughout his life. He wrote several long narrative poems, including *The Bothie of Tober-na-Vuolich* (1848) and *Amours de Voyage* (1858), which were well received but are now little read. A posthumous collection entitled simply *Poems* (1862) was a big success, and was reprinted 16 times over the next 40 years. It included his famous exposition of muscular Christianity, *Say not the struggle naught availeth*, and his satirical view of Victorian bourgeois morality in the lines 'Thou shalt not kill; but needst not strive Officiously to keep alive' from *The Latest Decalogue*. Clough's death from malaria while on a tour of Italy inspired Matthew Arnold to write his famous elegy *Thyrsis* in his memory.

Walt Whitman (1819–1892)

As a young man, Walt Whitman had spells as a printer, a teacher, a journalist, and an estate agent, publishing occasional stories and poems in newspapers with scant success. The first edition of *Leaves of Grass* (1855) received little notice, but Whitman continued to work on the poems, and produced a total of nine editions of the book during his lifetime, each containing more poems than the last. The ninth edition, published in the year of his death, contained over 400 poems, many of them originally condemned as obscene but now considered American classics. The books include war poems from two separate collections, *Drum Taps* and *Sequel to Drum Taps* (both 1865); the elegy on President Abraham Lincoln, *When Lilacs Last in the Dooryard Bloom'd*; inspirational verse such as *O Captain, My Captain!* and a body of sensual evocative, and occasionally mystical nature poetry. Whitman also published influential prose descriptions of the American Civil War, *Specimen Days and Collect* (1882).

Charles Baudelaire (1821–1867)

Charles Baudelaire, the son of a middle-ranking Parisian civil servant, abandoned a seafaring career after jumping ship in Mauritius, and lived off a family inheritance in his early twenties, squandering his money and spending much of the rest of his life in debt. His most important book, *Fleurs de Mal* (*Flowers of Evil*) (1857), now seen as one of the most important poetry collections of Nineteenth Century French literature, led to Baudelaire being fined and six of the poems being banned as indecent. The collection was reissued, without the offending poems but with new additions, in 1861 and posthumously in 1868. Baudelaire, often seen as the archetype of the self-indulgent and decadent artist, also published a collection of prose poems, *Petits Poèmes en Prose* (*Little Poems in Prose*) (1868).

Matthew Arnold (1822–1888)

Mathew Arnold spent most of his life as the Government's Inspector of Schools, travelling throughout the British Isles and Europe on official business. His first books of poetry, *The Strayed Reveller, and Other Poems* (1849) and *Empedocles on Etna, and Other Poems* (1852) appeared anonymously, but it was *Poems – A New Edition* (1853–4), published under his own name and including poems such as *The Scholar Gypsy* and *Sohrab and Rustum*, which first achieved critical notice. Arnold was appointed Professor of Poetry at Oxford University in 1857, and his poetic reputation was reinforced by *New Poems* (1867), which included *Dover Beach* and *Thyrsis*, his elegy on his friend Arthur Hugh Clough. Arnold is also important as a prose stylist, and the author of several classic works of religious, social and literary criticism, including *Culture and Anarchy* (1869) and *Literature and Dogma* (1873).

William (Johnson) Cory (1823–1892)

William Johnson, who took the surname Cory late in life after inheriting an estate, was a master at Eton College and a respected translator of Latin verse. He is remembered today for his elegy *Heraclitus* ('They told me, Heraclitus, they told me you were dead') translated from the Greek of Callimachus, which was included in his collection of largely homoerotic classical translations, *Ionica* (1858). Cory also wrote the words for the famous *Eton Boating Song* (1865).

Coventry Patmore (1823–1896)

Coventry Patmore worked for nearly 20 years as assistant librarian at the British Museum. His *Poems* (1844) sold very few copies, and Patmore bought up the rest and destroyed them. However, he continued to write poetry, and in 1854 produced the first part of his major work, *The Angel in the House* (1854–1862), a five-part novel in verse telling the story of love in a marriage. Soon after the publication of the final part, *The Victories of Love* (1862), his wife Emily died. Patmore's later verse, notably in *The Unknown Eros* (1877) was largely mystical and religious, and in his last years, he concentrated mainly on writing essays on literature, politics, and philosophy.

William McGonagall (1825–1902)

William McGonagall's poems, particularly *The Tay Bridge Disaster* (1880) are frequently mocked for their bizarre scansion and their grotesquely anticlimactic language:

> 'Beautiful Railway Bridge of the Silv'ry Tay!
> Alas! I am very sorry to say
> That ninety lives have been taken away
> On the last Sabbath day of 1879,
> Which will be remember'd for a very long time.'

McGonagall was a weaver in Dundee, and also worked as an actor at the town's Royal Theatre. He sold his poems – around two hundred of them – in broadsheets, and gave personal performances.

Dante Gabriel Rossetti (1828–1882)

Dante Gabriel Rossetti trained as a painter at the Royal Academy in London, and was one of the founders of the Pre-Raphaelite Brotherhood, which sought to revive the styles, themes, and colours of Medieval art. The son of an Italian poet and asylum-seeker and brother of the poet Christina Rossetti, he produced translations of Dante Alighieri and other Italian poets of the Middle Ages which were published in *The Early Italian Poets* (1861). He also wrote his own poetry, although much of it was unpublished when he decided to bury it in his wife's grave when she died in 1862. He was persuaded to retrieve the poems later, and they were eventually published as *Poems by D.G. Rossetti* (1870), causing much offence by their physical eroticism. This volume contained the first part of Rossetti's sonnet sequence, *The House of Life*, which was completed in *Ballads and Sonnets* (1881).

Rossetti also wrote several dramatic monologues – *The Last Confession* (1848), set in the Italian Risorgimento has been compared with the best of Robert Browning's work.

George Meredith (1828–1909)

George Meredith is known primarily as a novelist, although his early work, including *The Ordeal of Richard Feverel* (1859) met with little success, and he lived in poverty until later novels such as *The Egoist* (1879) and *Diana of the Crossways* (1885) achieved popularity. His first volume of verse, *Poems* (1851), made some impression, but *Modern Love* (1862), based on his own unhappy marriage and his wife's elopement, established a reputation which was enhanced by another nine volumes of poetry starting with *The Woods of Westermain* (1883) and including *Odes in Contribution to the Song of French History* (1898) and *A Reading of Life* (1901). His last years were blighted by ill-health, but Meredith was honoured as a great literary figure and elected to the Order of Merit.

Emily Dickinson (1830–1886)

Almost all of Emily Dickinson's poetry was written in secret, and only 10 of nearly 1,800 poems were published until after her death, when her sister gathered 115 in an edition entitled simply *Poems by Emily Dickinson* (1890). The success of this book led to *Poems: Second Series* (1891) and *Poems: Third Series* (1896). Emily Dickinson had lived a reclusive life in Amherst, Massachusetts, spending nearly 30 years caring for her ailing mother. Many of her poems were addressed to a mysterious and distant figure variously referred to as 'Sir' or 'Master', and there has been a lasting critical argument over whether these were addressed to a real or imaginary person. There is also a consistent religious theme running through her poetry.

Christina Georgina Rossetti (1830–1894)

Christina Rossetti was the younger sister of Dante Gabriel Rossetti, who illustrated her first book, *Goblin Market and Other Poems* (1862), and also *The Prince's Progress and Other Poems*, which followed it in 1866. These two volumes established her reputation as one of the leading poets of her day. She suffered from recurrent bouts of illness, but continued to publish religious and children's verse, notably *Sing-Song, a Nursery Rhyme Book* (1872) and *A Pageant and Other Poems* (1881). Her most famous poem, *In the Bleak Midwinter*, was published in a posthumous collection, *Poetic Works* (1896), and set to music as a Christmas carol in 1906.

Lewis Carroll (Charles Lutwidge Dodgson) (1832–1898)

Charles Lutwidge Dodgson was a shy, retiring Oxford mathematics lecturer who, under the pseudonym Lewis Carroll, produced some of the most original and evocative nonsense literature for children ever written. He is most famous for his two prose works, *Alice's Adventures in Wonderland* (1865) and *Through the Looking Glass* (1871), the latter including several famous nonsense poems, notably *Jabberwocky, Tweedledum and Tweedledee*, and *The Walrus and the Carpenter*. They feature many made-up words, some of which, such as 'chortle', have entered the language. Carroll also wrote *The Hunting of the Snark* (1874), as well as a number of minor poems and short stories, produced before *Alice* and published in small magazines and newspapers. As Charles Dodgson, he wrote several mathematics books.

James Thomson (1834–1882) (Bysshe Vanolis)

James Thomson, who wrote stories, essays, and poems under the pseudonym Bysshe Vanolis and is often distinguished from the earlier Scottish poet of the same name by the letters B.V. after his name, took to writing after being dismissed from the army for alcoholism. He is best known for *The City of Dreadful Night*, a long poem published in *The City of Dreadful Night and Other Poems* (1880),which presented an unremittingly bleak and hopeless view of contemporary urban life. He also translated the poems of the Italian poet Giacomo Leopardi.

William Morris (1834–1896)

The artist, illustrator, and interior designer William Morris, public-school and Oxford-educated son of a prosperous City of London broker, shared the nostalgia of Dante Gabriel Rossetti for the elegance and passion of Medieval art. His first published work, *The Defence of Guenevere and*

Other Poems (1858) was one of the earliest books clearly identifiable with the ideas of Rossetti's Pre-Raphaelite Brotherhood. However, it was not until the publication of the long narrative poem *The Life and Death of Jason* (1867) that he achieved success as a poet. His next book, *The Earthly Paradise* (1870), introduced Morris's fascination with the Icelandic sagas, several of which Morris later translated. His own imitation of the sagas, the epic *Story of Sigurd the Volsung and the Fall of the Niblungs* (1876) is considered one of his most important poetic works. In his last years, Morris wrote a series of prose romances and fantasies, including *The Well at the World's End* (1896). He was also a tireless campaigner for socialism and social equality.

Algernon Charles Swinburne (1837–1909)

Algernon Charles Swinburne was the son of an admiral, who provided him with an allowance that enabled him to follow a literary career after leaving Eton and Oxford University, where he had become close to Dante Gabriel Rossetti and the other members of the Pre-Raphaelite Brotherhood. Swinburne's first successful publication was the verse drama *Atalanta in Calydon* (1865), but it was *Poems and Ballads I* (1866) that brought him fame and notoriety. Victorian society was shocked by the explicit eroticism and masochism of many of the poems such as *Anactoria*. His next book, *Songs Before Sunrise* (1871) was heavily influenced by Swinburne's passionate commitment to Italian independence. Shortly after the publication of *Poems and Ballads II* (1878), Swinburne had a catastrophic mental breakdown, and spent the next 30 years in a nursing home. He continued to publish poetry, including the long epic *Tristram of Lyonesse* (1882), a re-telling of the love story of Tristram and Isolde, and the verse tragedy *Marino Faliero* (1885), but never regained his earlier revolutionary fire.

Bret Harte (1836–1902)

Bret Harte was an American writer and journalist who made himself unpopular by his outspoken condemnation of a massacre of Native Americans in California. He wrote poems and short stories for several magazines, first in California and later in New England. Among his most famous poems were *Dickens in Camp* (1870), which was written as a tribute on Dickens's death, and features a group of prospectors entranced by a reading from *The Old Curiosity Shop*, and *Plain Language from Truthful James* (1870), which describes a fight after a cheating game of cards. Harte's popularity declined after he moved east in 1871, and in his later years he was appointed to various diplomatic posts in Europe.

Wilfrid Scawen Blunt (1840–1922)

Wilfrid Scawen Blunt travelled extensively in the Middle East with his wife Lady Anne Blunt, the granddaughter of Lord Byron, and was an ardent supporter of Egyptian nationalism. Back in Britain, he campaigned for land reform in Ireland, and served two months in prison. Much of Blunt's love poetry, including the sonnet sequence *Esther*, is included in *Sonnets and Songs by Proteus* (1875 – 92). Apart from the strength of their passion and occasional nostalgic regret, they are notable for the evocation of the Sussex countryside where Blunt spent much of his life. He also wrote extensive political verse and translated several poems from Arabic. His *Collected Poems* was published in 1914.

Thomas Hardy (1840–1928)

Thomas Hardy's long life spanned the divide between the Victorian novel and the poetry of the modern age. He was born and brought up in the heart of the Dorset countryside where, under its ancient name of Wessex, he set his novels and much of his poetry. He was the son of a stonemason and small-time builder, and worked as a draughtsman for firms of architects in Dorset and London.

Disappointed by his failure to find a publisher for the poems he wrote as a young man – several of which he later revised to include in his first collection, *Wessex Poems and Other Verses* (1898) – he began writing prose fiction in his late twenties. He produced 14 of his highly-regarded Wessex novels, including *Far From the Madding Crowd* (1874), *The Mayor of Casterbridge* (1886) and *Tess of the D'Urbevilles* (1891), along with more than 40 short stories, but abandoned novel writing after the savage critical reception given to *Jude the Obscure* (1895).

Hardy had written poetry all his life but *Wessex Poems and Other Verses* published when he was 58, was his first major public appearance as a poet. From that date, all his publications, apart from a few short stories, a one-act play, and the three-part verse-drama *The Dynasts* (1904–1908), were collections of poetry, and practically every significant poet who followed him during the Twentieth Century owed a debt to them. Hardy's early life in rural Dorset had left him familiar with rural traditions and ways of life which had been unchanged for centuries – he used to play the violin with his father at country dances. Such customs were already vanishing as he grew up, but throughout his life he remained committed to the idea of celebrating and recording these links with the past. In 1874, he married Emma Gifford, the daughter of a parish rector in Cornwall, whom he had met while restoring her father's church. The marriage, after a four-year courtship, began happily although it was against the wishes of both their families, and they moved between London and Dorset while Hardy developed his literary career. With Emma's support, he had abandoned architecture in 1872 to work on the novel that would later become *Far From the Madding Crowd*.

Later, the couple became estranged, living largely separate lives for the last 20 years of Emma's life, and much of Hardy's love poetry became wistful and pensive. However, *Poems of the Past and Present* (1901) also included a series of highly original, sympathetic, and deeply personal war poems based on Hardy's understanding of the experiences of individual soldiers in the Boer War, including *Drummer Hodge* and *The Going of the Battery*.

Hardy, already a famous novelist, was now also a poet of international repute, although contemporary critics still did not rate his poetry as highly as his prose. He began work on *The Dynasts*, a hugely ambitious poetic drama mainly in blank verse, which tells the story of the Napoleonic Wars. Hardy strove for accuracy by interviewing old soldiers who had fought under Wellington and by visiting the battlefield at Waterloo. The story as Hardy told it reflected his personal philosophy of a universe controlled by an impassive and amoral Fate, which he referred to as the Immanent Will. This work, published in three volumes in 1903, 1905, and 1908, cemented Hardy's reputation. It was instrumental in achieving his appointment to the Order of Merit in 1910, shortly after the appearance of another collection of verse, *Time's Laughingstocks* (1909), which featured stories and characters from Hardy's Wessex background, along with a series of ballads and love lyrics.

Emma's death in 1912 inspired a fit of remorse and affection in Hardy; his grief, and a lengthy visit which he paid to the scene of their courtship in Cornwall, sparked an outpouring of some of his best work, much of it, including the 18 *Poems of 1912–13*, published in *Satires of Circumstance* (1914). Lyrics such as *Rain on a Grave, Beeny Cliff,* and *At Castle Boterel* revisit the marriage with deeply personal nostalgia and regret, while other poems in the volume, such as *The Convergence of the Twain,* written on the loss of the Titanic in 1912, or *Channel Firing,* marking the start of the First World War, demonstrate Hardy's more formal and public face.

Shortly after the publication of this collection, and still professing his devotion to his first wife, he married Florence Emily Dugdale, who was 38 years his junior. Hardy was now 74 years old, and, with Florence looking after all his material needs, he embarked on the remarkably productive final stage of his career. A volume of *Selected Poems* appeared in 1916, to be followed by three more collections of poetry, *Moments of Vision* (1917), *Late Lyrics and Earlier* (1922) and *Human Shows* (1925). His *Collected Poems* was published in 1919.

Hardy had expressed his wish to be buried with his parents, his grandparents, and his first wife at Stinsford, in Dorset, where he was born, but when he died in 1928 at Max Gate, the home he had built for himself and Emma in Dorchester more than 40 years before, there were demands that he should be commemorated in Poets' Corner in Westminster Abbey. Eventually his ashes were buried there, and his heart in a grave at Stinsford parish church. Many of Hardy's notebooks and personal papers were destroyed after his death, but a two volume account of the first 50 years of his life, *The Early Life of Thomas Hardy* (1928) and *The Later Years of Thomas Hardy* (1930), which he had largely compiled himself from his notes and diaries, was published by his widow.

Hardy's output was huge – apart from his novels and short stories and the three volumes of *The Dynasts,* he published about a thousand poems in eight volumes – and his range was considerable. His poetry includes occasional pieces, war poems, ballads, and love lyrics, and although his reputation slumped briefly in the years immediately following his death, he is recognised now as one of the most influential poets of the Twentieth Century.

Charles Montagu Doughty (1843–1926)

Charles Montagu Doughty was one of the greatest European explorers in Arabia, who described his wanderings in *Travels in Arabia Deserta* (1888), written in an idiosyncratic Elizabethan prose which alienated many readers at the time. After returning to Europe, Doughty wrote several verse plays, including *Adam Cast Forth* (1908), *The Cliffs* (1909) and *The Clouds* (1912) and a six-volume epic, *The Dawn in Britain* (1906), which describes the coming of Christianity to Britain. His final poem, *Mansoul. or the Riddle of the World* (1920), is an attempted philosophical study of religious belief. Despite the enthusiastic advocacy of T.E. Lawrence, none of Doughty's books sold well, and he lived a life of genteel poverty.

Robert Bridges (1844–1930)

Robert Bridges was a qualified doctor from a wealthy family, whose most important work was not published until his 85th birthday. Bridges's first book, *Poems*, was published in 1873, and was enlarged and republished several times over the years. It was followed by a sonnet sequence, *The Growth of Love* (1876), which enjoyed critical success, and shortly afterwards Bridges abandoned medicine to live on his private means and devote himself to poetry. He produced two long poems, *Prometheus the Firegiver* (1883) and *Eros and Psyche* (1885), and eight plays. His *Poetical Works* appeared in six volumes between 1898 and 1905, and in 1916 he published *The Spirit of Man*, an anthology of prose and verse which included six poems by Gerard Manley Hopkins, who was then almost unknown. Bridges took a particular interest in the mechanics and prosody of poetry, and *New Verse* (1925) contains much verse written in a metre based on syllables rather than stress, as is usual in English poetry. His greatest work, *The Testament of Beauty* (1929), a study of his spiritual philosophy, is also written in this form. Bridges was appointed Poet Laureate in 1913.

Paul Verlaine (1844–1896)

The French Symbolist poet Paul Verlaine, the only child of a wealthy French army officer, worked briefly as an insurance agent before publishing his first collection of poems, *Poèmes Saturniens* (*Poems of Saturn*) in 1866. The book was followed by *Fêtes Galantes* (*Gallant Celebrations*) (1869), and by the start of a long and turbulent relationship with the poet Arthur Rimbaud, which culminated in Verlaine's imprisonment in 1873 for wounding him with a revolver. Verlaine was a member of the French

Symbolist movement and published a number of other collections, notably *Romances sans Paroles* (*Affairs without Words*) (1874), *Sagesse* (*Wisdom*) (1880), and *Jadis et Naguère* (*Yesteryear and Yesterday*) (1884). He also wrote an influential series of studies of contemporary French poets, *Les Poètes Maudits* (*The accursed poets*) (1884).

Gerard Manley Hopkins (1844–1889)

Gerard Manley Hopkins studied classics at Oxford University, where he achieved a considerable reputation as a poet. He burned much of his early poetry when he decided to become a Jesuit in 1868, although he asked his friend Robert Bridges to look after some copies. He devoted himself to religious studies for the next few years, but was inspired to write poetry again by the sinking of the ferry *Deutschland* in 1875. *The Wreck of the Deutschland*, written the following year, was not published until after his death, like most of his poems. Much of Hopkins's poetry combines strong religious feeling with a thinly disguised homoerotic passion. The so-called 'terrible sonnets', written at a time of deep philosophical despair, are among his most powerful works, although poems such as *God's Grandeur* and *The Windhover* are also well known. He devised an irregular system of prosody for many of his poems, known as 'sprung rhythm', which allows any number of unstressed syllables in a line. Hopkins's poetry was first published in 1918 by the then Poet Laureate, Robert Bridges, and he slowly came to be accepted as one of the most original and important poets of his era.

Andrew Lang (1844–1912)

Andrew Lang, a Scottish scholar born at Selkirk, is best known today for his collections of traditional fairy tales, which appeared in 12 volumes between 1889 and 1910. He was a leading authority on anthropology and folklore, producing important books such as *Custom and Myth* (1884) and *Myth, Ritual and Religion* (1887). As a poet, Lang published *The Ballads and Lyrics of Old France* (1872), a collection of verse that was most remarkable for its use of unusual French forms and metres, and followed it with several other collections of ballads and other traditional poems. After his ambitious long narrative poem, *Helen of Troy* (1882) failed to achieve any success he restricted himself mainly to light verse. His *Collected Poems* (1923) was published posthumously.

Edmund Gosse (1849–1928)

Sir Edmund Gosse had a distinguished career as a literary and art critic, and produced translations of Ibsen's plays which were instrumental in introducing the playwright to English audiences. In addition to influential works of art criticism, several books on English poetry, and a highly regarded autobiographical memoir, *Father and Son* (1907), he published a number of books of his own poems, notably *On Viol and Flute* (1873) and *New Poems* (1879). Gosse was a close friend of Swinburne and the Pre-Raphaelites, whose influence appears in the lush imagery and erotic richness of his *Collected Poems* (1896).

Alice Meynell (1847–1922)

Alice Meynell (née Thompson) was a convert to Roman Catholicism much of whose poetry was concerned with religious meditation. Her first book, *Preludes* (1875), which includes the sonnet *Renunciation*, received little critical attention, but she continued to write poetry alongside a successful career as a journalist and editor and as the author of a number of books on literature. *Later Poems* (1902) and *Last Poems*, published posthumously in 1923, gradually won her a considerable reputation. She was also a dedicated and active supporter of the suffragette movement to win women's right to vote.

W.E. Henley (1849–1903)

William Ernest Henley's life was plagued by illness, and his poetic career began with a series of poems, *Hospital Sketches* (1875), written while he was recovering from the amputation of his left foot and published some years later. As a journalist and editor, he was known as a champion of modern artists including James McNeill Whistler and Auguste Rodin, and as a literary critic who encouraged writers such as Rudyard Kipling and H.G. Wells. His friend Robert Louis Stevenson is said to have based his *Treasure Island* character Long John Silver on the one-legged Henley. His books of poetry included *A Book of Verses* (1888), *London Voluntaries*

(1893), *Poems* (1898), and *For England's Sake* (1900). Henley is known for his muscular patriotism and for the inspirational defiance of the famous lines from *Invictus* (1875): 'I am the master of my fate, I am the captain of my soul.'

Robert Louis Stevenson (1850–1894)

Robert Louis Stevenson, often referred to simply as RLS, was an essayist and author as well as a poet – *Treasure Island, Kidnapped, Catriona*, and *The Strange case of Dr Jekyll and Mr Hyde* are among his most famous books. As a poet, he is best known for *A Child's Garden of Verses* (1885), a sentimental collection of children's poems set largely in a Victorian nursery. Among them are *The Lamplighter, Keepsake Mill*, and *From a Railway Carriage*.

Arthur Rimbaud (1854–1891)

Along with Paul Verlaine and Charles Baudelaire, Arthur Rimbaud was one of the most important French Symbolist poets. His torrid homosexual relationship with Paul Verlaine, fuelled by debauchery, drink and drugs, scandalised literary Paris and was reflected in his collections of prose poems *Une Saison en Enfer* (*A Season in Hell*) (1873) and *Les Illuminations*, (*The Illuminations*) (1874). By then, Rimbaud had already published *Poesies* (*Verses*) (1869) and *Le Bateau Ivre* (*The Drunken Boat* (1871), a 100-line poem of shocking, luxurious, and mystical images which describes the sinking of a boat at sea as it fills with water. In 1875, after a bitter parting with Verlaine, Rimbaud abandoned poetry. He died of cancer 16 years later, at the age of 37.

Oscar Wilde (1854–1900)

Oscar Wilde, the flamboyant and extravagant son of a respected Dublin surgeon, was one of the most brilliant students of his day at Trinity College Dublin and Oxford, winning Oxford University's Newdigate Prize for his poem, *Ravenna* (1878). His glittering aestheticism, brilliant wit, and outspoken contempt for conventional attitudes made him a famous but controversial figure as a young man. *Poems* (1881) shows the influences of Rossetti and the Pre-Raphaelite Brotherhood poets, and was followed by a lecture tour of the United States. Wilde wrote several successful society comedies during the 1890s, of which the most famous was *The Importance of Being Earnest* (1895), in which his gift for producing witty and often scandalous one-liners was given full rein. He also wrote a melodramatic novel, *The Picture of Dorian Gray* (1890), and demonstrated a remarkable talent for fairy stories and allegories in *The Happy Prince and Other Tales* (1888), which was written for his sons. But his greatest work came after his trial and conviction on charges of gross indecency with other men. *The Ballad of Reading Gaol* (1898) abandons his expansive but often brittle witticisms for a deceptively simple and straightforward style, and describes the effect of the execution of a convicted murderer on the other prisoners in the gaol. Wilde died in exile in France two years after its anonymous publication.

John Meade Falkner (1858–1932)

John Meade Falkner, a successful teacher and later a businessman who headed a leading arms manufacturing company during the First World War, is best known today for his novel *Moonfleet* (1898). Apart from two other novels, he also wrote poetry throughout his life, largely concerned with history and ancient religious institutions. Much of it was published posthumously in *Poems* (1933).

A.E. Housman (1859–1936)

Alfred Edward Housman, although a brilliant classicist at Oxford, failed his final examinations and spent 10 years as a clerk in London, before being appointed Professor of Latin at London University. *A Shropshire Lad* (1896), his first collection of poems, was published at his own expense but failed to make much impression until the Great War, when it became hugely popular. He produced another collection, *Last Poems* (1922), which dealt with similar themes of death, disillusion, and failure in a characteristic mood of regretful stoicism. By this time, Housman had moved to Cambridge University. *More Poems* (1936), collected from his notebooks by his brother, appeared after his death and his *Collected Poems* (1939) followed three years later.

Francis Thompson (1859–1907)

Francis Thompson spent three years as a homeless opium addict in London, writing poetry which he submitted to a Roman Catholic magazine run by the husband of the poet Alice Meynell. Meynell and her husband encouraged him to continue writing, and arranged for the publication of his first book, *Poems* (1893), which was followed by two more books of intensely religious verse. His most famous poem was *The Hound of Heaven* (1890), which pictures God hunting down the human soul, but he also wrote the much gentler and nostalgic cricket poem, *At Lord's* (1908). Thompson's health was permanently damaged by his opium addiction, and he died of tuberculosis at the age of 48.

Sir Henry Newbolt (1862–1938)

Sir Henry Newbolt was a barrister and novelist who also became famous as the author of stirring patriotic ballads and poems such as *Drake's Drum* and *Vitaï Lampada* (*The Torch of Life*), both published in *Admirals All and Other Verses* (1897). *Vitaï Lampada* in particular, with its rousing injunction to 'Play up, play up, and play the game' enjoyed huge popularity, although Newbolt later said that continued requests to recite it sometimes made him feel that he had created a Frankenstein's monster. More of Newbolt's poetry, much of it nautical and inspirational, was published in *Poems Old and New* (1912), catching the mood of eager patriotism at the start of the First World War. Newbolt was knighted in 1915, after being recruited to help maintain public morale during the war, and later served as comptroller of wireless and cables. He also wrote the official naval history of the war, and was appointed a Companion of Honour in 1922.

Rudyard Kipling (1865–1936)

Rudyard Kipling was born in British-ruled India, and returned there as a young man after an unhappy childhood in England to work as a journalist. Memories of India inform many of the short stories he started to write – he brought out six volumes between 1887 and 1889 – and also the novel *Kim* (1901). Kipling also published *Barrack Room Ballads* (1892) a collection which sought to depict the lives and feelings of ordinary British soldiers through poems such as *Danny Deever*, *Gunga Din*, and *Mandalay*. Other collections of poetry and short stories followed, among them the two *Jungle Books* (1894–1895), *The Seven Seas* (1896) and *Rewards and Fairies* (1909), which included his famous poem *If*, which he later complained had been 'anthologised to weariness'. *Recessional*, Kipling's sombre forecast of the eventual decline of the British Empire he loved, was written to mark Queen Victoria's Diamond Jubilee in 1897. Today, poems such as *Recessional* or *The White Man's Burden* (1899) seem to demonstrate a short-sighted imperialism, but the death in the First World War of Kipling's son Jack revealed a more sensitive, vulnerable character. His elegy, *My Boy Jack* was published in 1915, and in his collection *The Years Between* (1919), he wrote an epitaph for the fallen soldiers of the War:

'If any question why we died,
Tell them, Because our fathers lied.'

Kipling was also responsible for the suggestion that 'Known Unto God' should be inscribed on unidentified graves in war cemeteries. In 1907, he became the first British writer to be awarded the Nobel Prize for Literature.

W.B. Yeats (1865–1939)

William Butler Yeats, the Irish poet, dramatist, prose writer and nationalist, was born in Sandymount, Dublin, although his family moved to London when he was two years old, and his early education was at the Godolphin School, Hammersmith. However, regular visits to his grandparents' home in Sligo, in western Ireland, fostered a passionate interest in Irish scenery, folklore, and mythology, and at the age of 15 he moved with his parents back to Dublin.

Yeats's father, John Butler Yeats, was a former barrister who had forged a new career as a portrait painter, and his brother, Jack Yeats, also established a reputation as a painter and illustrator. Yeats himself studied at the School of Art in Dublin, but in 1887, two years after the appearance of his first published poems, two short lyrics in the *Dublin University Review*, he decided to devote himself to writing. By this time, he was back in London, where he worked on the early poems eventually published as *The Wanderings of Oisin, and Other Poems* (1889). Other early collections, many of the poems dealing with mysticism and Irish mythology and history, included *The Secret Rose* (1897) and *The Wind Among the Reeds* (1899).

In Dublin, he had established a lasting connection with the poet George William Russell (AE), who encouraged his growing interest in mysticism and the supernatural, and in London he developed his friendship with other poets such as Lionel Johnson, Ernest Dowson, and Richard Le Gallienne in the Rhymers' Club, which he helped to establish. He also became increasingly involved with séances, mysticism and the occult, and his work on the preparation of a complete edition of the works of William Blake reinforced his commitment to a visionary and mystical view of the world.

In 1889, he met the Irish beauty and ardent nationalist Maud Gonne, and fell passionately in love with her. Although she did not return his feelings, and despite his disillusionment with politics, Yeats's love for her was a powerful encouragement to his own Irish nationalism. He helped to found an Irish Literary Society in London in 1891 and another in Dublin the following year. Maud Gonne played the lead in his play *Cathleen ni Houlihan* (1902), helping to establish the new Irish National Theatre Company, which acquired the Abbey Theatre in Dublin. In 1893, Yeats produced a volume of essays, *The Celtic Twilight*, and along with Augusta, Lady Gregory and other playwrights such as J.M. Synge, Sean O'Casey, and George Bernard Shaw, became one of the most influential figures in the Irish Revival.

He was still producing poetry alongside the plays which he was writing for the Abbey Theatre, and further collections, including *In the Seven Woods* (1903), *The Green Helmet and Other Poems* (1910), and *The Wild Swans at Coole* (1919) show Yeats moving away from the lush Pre-Raphaelite atmosphere and imagery of his early work in favour of a new spare expression and restrained imagery. One of his best-known poems, *Easter 1916*, was written in response to the execution of nationalist leaders of the Easter Rising, including Maud Gonne's husband, John MacBride. Published in *Michael Robartes and the Dancer* (1921), it includes Yeats's famous lines,

> 'All changed, changed utterly:
> A terrible beauty is born.'

In 1917, having been finally turned down both by Maud Gonne and by her daughter Iseult, he married the occultist Georgie Hyde-Lees, who at 24 was 28 years his junior. He was now reaching the summit of his achievement, and the award of the Nobel Prize for Literature in December 1923 was followed by a succession of new books of some of his greatest poetry.

At the same time, however, he began to take an active role in the political life of the newly-formed Irish Free State. He became a Senator in 1922, and, arguing as a Protestant against the overwhelming influence of the Catholic Church in the new state, conducted a passionate campaign against proposals to outlaw divorce. But his main interests remained philosophical and literary: universally accepted as one of the most significant contemporary poets, he was asked to make a selection of the most important poetry of the late Nineteenth and early Twentieth Century for the massively influential *Oxford Book of Modern Verse* (1936).

Yeats's wife's interest in 'automatic writing' as a way of contacting the spirit world had led to the writing of *A Vision* (1925), a prose study of philosophy, astrology, the occult, and poetry which he later described as his 'book of books'. It helped him to develop the complex theories of a constant cyclic reworking of history and the wide-ranging system of symbolism which became increasingly important in his later poetry collections such as *The Tower* (1928), *The Winding Stair* (1933), *New Poems* (1938) and *Last Poems and Two Plays* (1939).

Yeats remained committed to the history, traditions, and rural life of Ireland. He bought a ruined Norman castle, Thoor Ballylee, near to Lady Gregory's family home at Coole Park, County Galway, which became the recurrent symbol of the Tower in his poetry. In *Under Ben Bulben*, the final poem of *Last Poems and Two Plays*, Yeats had described the simple grave he envisaged for himself in the churchyard at Drumcliff in Sligo, where, he said, an ancestor had once been rector. However, he died while on a trip to France in January 1939, and was buried after a ceremony in Roquebrune, on the French Riviera. After the Second World War, his body was moved to Sligo and buried as he had wished, under the epitaph he had written for himself:

'Cast a cold eye
On life, on death.
Horseman, pass by!'

Richard Le Gallienne (1866–1947)

Richard Le Gallienne was born in Liverpool, and studied as an accountant for seven years before leaving to live in London as a writer. There, he associated with W.B. Yeats, Oscar Wilde, Lionel Johnson, Ernest Dowson, and other members of the Rhymers' Club, which met in the capital and published anthologies of verse in the late Nineteenth Century. His first publication, *My Ladies' Sonnets and Other Vain and Amatorious Verses* (1887) was followed by several works of literary criticism and many books of poetry, including a translation of *The Rubaiyat of Omar Khayyam* (1897), which he described as 'a paraphrase from several literal translations'. Apart from his poetry, he wrote a novel, *The Quest of the Golden Girl* (1896), and two volumes of autobiographical memoir, *The Romantic 90s* (1926) and *From a Paris Garrett* (1936). Le Gallienne moved to the United States in 1901, and lived there and in the South of France for the rest of his life.

Lionel Johnson (1867–1902)

Lionel Johnson was a convert to Roman Catholicism who was an influential literary critic in the 1890s when his *The Art of Thomas Hardy* (1894) was one of the earliest detailed studies of Hardy's novels. Johnson was a member of the London-based Rhymers' Club, with W.B. Yeats, Oscar Wilde, and others. His *Poems* (1895) and *Ireland and Other Poems* (1897) include a number of gentle and evocative lyrics which show the influence of his fervent Catholic faith, among them *By the Statue of King Charles at Charing Cross* and the threatening *The Dark Angel*. Johnson, who struggled throughout his life with alcoholism and ill-health, died in his mid-thirties after a fall in a London street.

George William Russell (AE) (1867–1935)

George William Russell, who wrote under the pseudonym AE (sometimes written Æ), was a dedicated Irish nationalist and a poet, artist, and mystic who was considered early in his career to be at least the equal of his friend W.B. Yeats. His first book, *Homeward: Songs by the Way* (1894) established his reputation as a writer of mystical poetry which drew heavily on Celtic history and tradition, and he continued to publish poetry throughout his life. *The Divine Vision* (1904), *Gods of War* (1915), *The*

Interpreters (1922) and *Midsummer Eve* (1928) are among his most important works. His *Collected Poems* appeared in 1913. As an Irish nationalist, Russell was an active supporter of agricultural reform through the co-operative movement, and from 1923 to 1930 he edited *The Irish Statesman*, a literary and political magazine supporting the newly independent Irish state. Russell was also a spiritualist and clairvoyant.

Lawrence Binyon (1869–1943)

Lawrence Binyon, who was born into a Quaker family in Lancashire, left Oxford University to work in the British Museum, where he remained for most of his career. He published several books of poetry, including *Lyric Poems* (1894), *Odes* (1901), and *The New World* (1918), a translation of Dante (1933–1943), several plays, and a large number of critical books on western and oriental art and literature. His *Collected Poems* was published in two volumes in 1931. Binyon served with a military ambulance unit during the First World War. His most famous poem, published in *The Times* newspaper in 1914, is *For the Fallen*, which includes the line made famous on thousands of war memorials, 'They shall grow not old, as we that are left grow old.'

T. Sturge Moore (1870–1944)

Thomas Moore, who took the name Sturge to distinguish himself from the Irish satirist and poet who wrote *Lalla Rookh*, was a poet, playwright, engraver, and book illustrator who was a great friend of W.B. Yeats. His first book of poetry, *The Vinedresser and Other Poems* (1899) was followed by more than 30 plays and verse dramas, including several showing the influences of the highly stylised Japanese Noh drama, and also by several other volumes of poetry and prose. He was also a noted art critic, and as an engraver and designer produced bookplates and bindings for Yeats and other poets.

Hilaire Belloc (1870–1953)

Hilaire Belloc was born in France, the son of a French father and an English mother, but was educated in England, becoming a naturalised British subject in 1902 and serving briefly as a Member of Parliament. He is particularly known today for his books of nonsense verse for children, *The Bad Child's Book of Beasts* (1896), *More Beasts for Worse Children* (1897), *Cautionary Tales* (1907) and *New Cautionary Tales* (1930). However, Belloc was a prolific writer who produced over a hundred and fifty books, including novels, essays and works of poetry, history, religion and travel. Among his volumes of poetry are *Verses and Sonnets* (1896), *The Modern Traveller* (1898) and *Sonnets and Verses* (1923). Belloc was an ardent campaigner for the Roman Catholic church and a close friend of G.K. Chesterton, who illustrated several of his books and shared not only his Catholic faith but also his deep-rooted distrust of modern industrial society.

J.M. Synge (1871–1909)

John Millington Synge was an Irish playwright, who spent several years in the remote Aran Islands off the west coast of Ireland, later publishing his journal as *The Aran Islands* (1907). Synge wrote six plays between 1903 and his death in 1909, the most famous of which, *The Playboy of the Western World* (1907) caused riots in Dublin because of its perceived attack on the Irish character. His poetry, much of it showing the influence of his friend W.B. Yeats and reflecting his interest in Celtic history and mythology, appeared in several magazines and was published in *Poems and Translations* (1909). Synge, one of the co-founders of Dublin's Abbey Theatre, suffered from ill health for much of his life, and died of cancer at the age of 37.

W.H. Davies (1871–1940)

William Henry Davies was born in South Wales, but spent several years as a tramp in the United States, supporting himself by taking casual work and crossing the Atlantic several times on cattle ships. An accident while trying to jump onto a moving freight train led to the amputation of his left leg, and Davies returned to live on the streets in London. He wrote a prose account of his wanderings in *Autobiography of a Super-Tramp* (1907). His first book of poetry, *The Soul's Destroyer* (1905) was published at his own expense, and attracted the attention of several influential poets and critics, including Edward Thomas. Later books, including *Nature Poems* (1908), *Forty New Poems* (1918), *Ambition and Other Poems* (1929), *Poems 1930–31* (1931), and *The Loneliest Mountain* (1939) won him widespread

THE FIRST BOOK

OF

THE FAERIE QUEENE

CONTAYNING

THE LEGEND OF THE KNIGHT OF THE RED CROSSE, OR
OF HOLINESSE.

I.

LO! I, the man whose Muse whylome did maske,
As time her taught, in lowly shepheards weeds,[1]
Am now enforst, a farre unfitter taske,
For trumpets sterne to chaunge mine oaten reeds,
And sing of Knights and Ladies gentle deeds;
Whose praises having slept in silence long,
Me, all too meane, the sacred Muse areeds[2]
To blazon broade emongst her learned throng:
Fierce warres and faithful loves shall moralize my song.

II.

Help then, O holy virgin, chiefe of nyne,
Thy weaker novice to perform thy will;
Lay forth out of thine everlasting scryne[3]
The antique rolles, which there lye hidden still,
Of Faerie Knights, and fayrest Tanaquill[*]

[1] *Weeds*, clothes.   [2] *Areeds*, teaches.
[3] *Scryne*, (*scrinium*, Lat.,) a cabinet in which papers were kept.
[*] *Tanaquill* is another name for Gloriana, the Faerie Queene.

3*

Edmund Spenser's *The Faerie Queene* dressed Tudor England in the clothes of mediaeval knightly chivalry. *Photo by Pat Roberts*

William Shakespeare's statue stands in Leicester Square, in the middle of London's Theatreland.

TO THE RIGHT HONORABLE HENRIE WRIOTHESLEY, EARLE OF SOUTH-AMPTON, AND BARON OF TITCHFIELD.

RIGHT HONOURABLE, I know not how I shall offend in dedicating my vnpolisht lines to your Lordship, nor how the worlde will censure mee for choosing so strong a proppe to support so weake a burthen, onelye if your Honour seeme but pleased, I account my selfe highly praised, and vowe to take aduantage of all idle houres, till I haue honoured you with some grauer labour. But if the first heire of my inuention proue deformed, I shall be sorie it had so noble a god-father: and neuer after eare so barren a land, for feare it yeeld me still so bad a haruest. I leaue it to your Honourable suruey, and your Honor to your hearts content, which I wish may alwaies answere your owne wish, and the worlds hopefull expeĉtation.

Your Honors in all dutie,
WILLIAM SHAKESPEARE.

Venus and Adonis was dedicated to Henry Wriothesley (pronounced Risley), 3rd Earl of Southampton. *Photo by Pat Roberts*

John Milton fled London in 1665 to escape the plague, and lived in this cottage in Chalfont St Giles, Buckinghamshire. He is said to have worked on *Paradise Lost*, first published two years later, while living here.

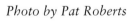

Photo by Pat Roberts

A statue of John Bunyan, holding a copy of *The Pilgrim's Progress*, stands in a niche high above the pavement near the scene of his death in Holborn, London.

The house of the Eighteenth Century poet John Dryden is now at the heart of London's Chinatown. *Photo by Pat Roberts*

THE
MISCELLANEOUS WORKS
OF
JOHN DRYDEN, Esq;
CONTAINING ALL HIS
ORIGINAL POEMS, TALES,
AND
TRANSLATIONS.
Now first Collected and Published together
IN FOUR VOLUMES.
WITH
EXPLANATORY NOTES AND OBSERVATIONS,
ALSO AN
ACCOUNT OF HIS LIFE AND WRITINGS.
VOLUME THE FIRST.
LONDON:
Printed for J. and R. TONSON, in the Strand,
MDCCLX.

JOHN DRYDEN

A N

E S S A Y on *M A N.*

E P I S T L E I.

WAKE! my LÆLIUS, leave all meaner Things
To low Ambition and the Pride of Kings.
Let Us (since Life can little more supply
Than juſt to look about us, and to die)
Expatiate free, o'er all this *Scene of Man,*   5
A mighty Maze! but not without a Plan;
A Wild, where weeds and flowers promiſcuous ſhoot,
Or Garden, tempting with forbidden fruit.

2   Toge-

Pope's *Essay on Man* appeared in 1732. *Photo by Pat Roberts*

Samuel Johnson's house in the City of London features a statue of his much-loved cat, Hodge.

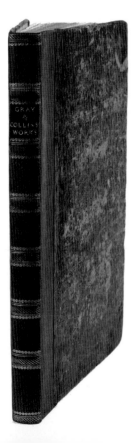

The works of Thomas Gray and William Collins were often bound together. This edition was published in 1787. *Photo by Pat Roberts*

Versions of this statue of Robert Burns by the Victorian sculptor John Steell stand in London, Dundee, and Central Park, New York.

Samuel Taylor Coleridge moved to this house in Kensington, West London, in 1810. *The Rime of the Ancient Mariner*, commemorated in 2003 by a statue by Alan Herriot in Watchet Harbour, Somerset, had appeared in 1798.

Photo by Peter Murphy, Watchet

The statue of Thomas Chatterton, who was born in St Mary Redcliffe, Bristol, now sits in the city's Millennium Square.
Photo by Richard Bretton

Charles Lamb lived in this six-room cottage in Islington, North London, with his sister Mary for 10 years from 1823. A memorial to the man once described as the most lovable figure in English literature is in the City of London.

Fine editions of the extensive works of Percy Bysshe Shelley, such as this ten-volume edition of 1926-30, appeared throughout the nineteenth and twentieth centuries. He lived at this house in Marlow, Buckinghamshire, before leaving in 1818 for Italy, where he died four yeasr later. Photo by Pat Roberts

The Poet & Playwrig[ht]
PERCY BYSSHE SHELLEY
and his wife MARY
authoress of 'Frankenstein'
lived here
1817 - 1818

R.C. Belt's nine-foot statue of Lord Byron, next to London's Hyde Park, was erected in 1881. Belt was inspired by a line from Byron's *Childe Harold*, 'To sit on rocks, to muse o'er flood and fell.'

Wentworth Place, the Hampstead House owned by Keats's friend Charles Brown, where the poet lived, fell in love with Fanny Brawne, and wrote some of his most memorable poetry.

This fine edition of John Keats's *Lamia* was published in 1928.

ELIZABETH BARRETT BROWNING
1806-1861
·POET·
LIVED IN A HOUSE
ON THIS SITE
1838-1846

The house in Wimpole Street, London from which Elizabeth Barrett eloped to become Elizabeth Barrett Browning has been demolished, but its site is still marked by a stone memorial.

At the request

of

Messrs *BOUSSOD, VALADON & C°*

and

for the sake

of

my old friend

EDWARD LEAR

I sign

these hundred proof copies

Tennyson

This portrait of Tennyson is taken from an 1889 edition of his poems dedicated to Edward Lear.
Photos by Pat Roberts

The Owl and the Pussy-cat went to sea
In a beautiful pea-green boat,

EDWARD LEAR • 1812-1888

The Owl and the Pussycat was one of four of Edward Lear's poems featured on postage stamps to mark the centenary of his death in 1988.

Emily Brontë and her sisters Charlotte and Anne were brought up in the parsonage in the West Yorkshire village of Haworth.

Maggi Hambling's statue, *A Conversation with Oscar Wilde*, was unveiled in London in 1998.

D.G. Rossetti lived in this house, then on the bank of the Thames, with his brother William and his fellow poet A.C. Swinburne. He kept a bizarre menagerie of animals in the house, including parrots, wombats, peacocks and an armadillo.

DANTE GABRIEL
ROSSETTI
1828 - 1882
AND
ALGERNON CHARLES
SWINBURNE
1837 - 1909
lived here

LONDON COUNTY COUNCIL

A.E. Housman, though famous for his lyrics set in the Shropshire countryside, hardly ever visited the county. This is the house in North London where he wrote many of the poems in *A Shropshire Lad*.

Hilaire Belloc moved into his Chelsea home overlooking the Thames in 1899, soon after returning to Britain with his American wife, Elodie Hogan.

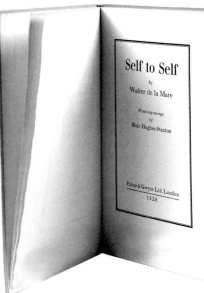

Walter de la Mare's *Self to Self* was one of over a hundred books of poetry and stories published during his lifetime. *Photo by Pat Roberts*

G.K. Chesterton grew up in London's fashionable Kensington, and lived here until his marriage in 1901.

James Elroy Flecker, who died at the age of 30, was born in this undistinguished house in the London suburb of Lewisham.

The Marlow, Buckinghamshire house in which T.S. Eliot and his wife Vivien lived while he was working in a London bank is now a restaurant.

Siegfried Sassoon had an attic flat in this Holland Park house. He warned the elderly Sir Henry Newbolt, when he visited in 1927, that there were 52 stairs to climb.

ENGLISH HERITAGE
ISAAC ROSENBERG
1890~1918
Poet and Painter
lived in the East End
and studied here

Isaac Rosenberg was brought up in poverty in London's East End. After leaving school at the age of 14, he spent much of his spare time studying in the Whitechapel library.

A seven-foot bronze statue of John Betjeman stands in London's St Pancras Station, which he was instrumental in saving from demolition in the 1960s.

Louis MacNeice lived in this house in Islington, London, for part of the time when he was working as a BBC producer.

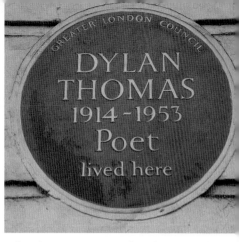

After he came to London from South Wales, Dylan Thomas lived for a while in a basement flat in this house in Camden, North London. He wrote: 'When I do come to town, bang go my plans in a horrid alcoholic explosion.'

Ted Hughes, Poet Laureate from 1984 to 1998, was born in a little cottage in Mytholmroyd, West Yorkshire. His wife, the American poet Sylvia Plath, was buried in the local churchyard after her suicide in 1963.

popularity as a strikingly original lyric poet with a passionate love of nature. His most famous poem, *Leisure*, appeared in *Songs of Joy and Others* (1911). Davies gave many popular public readings of his work, but continued to live as a recluse for most of his life.

Ralph Hodgson (1871–1962)

Ralph Hodgson was born in Yorkshire, but grew up in London, where he became a journalist and publisher and the friend and confidant of poets such as Walter de la Mare, Siegfried Sassoon, and T.S. Eliot. His first book of poetry, *The Last Blackbird* (1907), introduced his lifelong themes of England and nature, which developed through his later books, *Eve* (1913) and *Poems* (1917). Hodgson's best-known and most anthologised poems are sentimental verses with simple rhythms, such as *Time, You Old Gypsy Man* and *The Bells of Heaven* (both 1917), but *The Bull* (1913) demonstrates his clear-sighted view of the cruelty of nature. His passionate anger flares out in *To Deck a Woman*, a long poem about the exploitation of animals by the fashion trade. Hodgson lectured on English literature in Japan for 14 years until 1938, and then lived in the United States. He published a further volume of poetry, *The Skylark and Other Poems* (1958) after a silence of more than 40 years, and his *Collected Poems* appeared in 1961.

John Cowper Powys (1872–1963)

John Cowper Powys, who claimed descent on his mother's side from William Cowper, was born in Derbyshire but spent much of his life as a teacher and lecturer in the United States. He is best known for his *Autobiography* (1934) and for his many novels, particularly *A Glastonbury Romance* (1932) and *Owen Glendower* (1940), but his writing career began with a volume of poetry, *Odes and Other Poems* (1896). Another collection, *Samphire* (1922), was published in the United States, and a third volume, *Lucifer* (1956) was written in 1906 but not published for 50 years.

Walter de la Mare (1873–1956)

Walter de la Mare began writing poetry and short stories while working as a bookkeeper and statistician at the Anglo-American Oil Company in London. His first book, *Songs of Childhood* (1902), published under the pseudonym Walter Ramal, was aimed at children, and much of his later career was marked by a fascination for the richness of the child's emotion and imagination. In 1908, having been granted a Civil List pension, he left the oil company and devoted himself to writing. Later collections included *The Listeners* (1912) and *Peacock Pie* (1913), and several volumes of poetry for adults, including *The Burning Glass* (1945) and *O Lovely England* (1953). De la Mare also wrote five novels and a number of collections of short stories and edited an influential anthology of poetry and prose, *Come Hither* (1923).

G.K. Chesterton (1874–1936)

Gilbert Keith Chesterton was a prolific author of essays, short stories, literary criticism, biographies, history, fantasy and – with his famous character Father Brown – detective fiction. But his first two published books, *Greybeards at Play* and *The Wild Knight and Other Poems* (both 1900) were both poetry collections, and he went on to write several hundred poems, described by T.S. Eliot as 'first-rate journalistic balladry', which appeared in magazines, anthologies, and other collections. Many, such as *The Rolling English Road* (1913) or *The Ballad of the White Horse* (1911) expressed a boisterous and beery patriotism; others, such as *The Donkey* (1900) were products of Chesterton's deeply-felt Catholic faith. Some, like *Elegy in a Country Churchyard* (1922) and *For the Creche* (1919) demonstrate his biting wit and disaffection for modern life and politics, while his best-known poem, *Lepanto* (1915) celebrates the triumph of Christian Europe over the Turks in 1571. Chesterton's *Collected Poems* appeared in 1927, to be followed by *New and Collected Poems* two years later.

Robert Service (1874–1958)

Robert Service, who is sometimes known as the 'Canadian Kipling' was born in Lancashire, but emigrated to Canada as a young man to work in a bank. Many of his most famous ballads, such as *The Shooting of Dan McGrew* (1907) were developed from stories he heard of the gold rush in the Yukon in the 1890s, and *The Spell of the Yukon and Other Verses* (1907), published in England as *The Songs of a Sourdough*, was a major success, enabling Service to leave the bank and travel as a writer, spending most of his time in Europe. Work as an ambulance driver in the First World War led to *Rhymes of a Red Cross Man* (1916), which was followed by several other collections of poetry about explorers and pioneers, set in various parts of the world including South Africa and Afghanistan. Service also wrote several novels and two volumes of autobiography, *Ploughman of the Moon* (1945) and *Harper of Heaven* (1948).

Robert Frost (1874–1963)

Robert Frost was born and brought up in the United States, where he worked at various times as a teacher and a poultry farmer, while continuing to write poetry which he could not persuade anyone to publish. At the age of 38, he moved with his family to Britain, where his first collection, *A Boy's Will* (1913) appeared. He became friends with several leading poets, including Ezra Pound, T.E. Hulme, and Edward Thomas, and published another successful book of poetry, *North of Boston* (1914) before returning to the US, where *North of Boston* became a best-seller. Frost bought a farm and began a career of writing, teaching, and lecturing, producing *Mountain Interval* (1916) and *New Hampshire* (1923), which won the first of four Pulitzer Prizes presented to him during his lifetime. Other collections included *West Running Brook* (1928), *A Further Range* (1936), *A Witness Tree* (1942), *Steeple Bush* (1947) and *In the Clearing* (1962). Frost's poetry, with its avoidance of traditional verse forms, its frequently bleak view of nature, and its incisive command of the colloquial speech of ordinary people, charted a new direction for American literature.

Edward Thomas (1878–1917)

Edward Thomas was born in London of Welsh parents. He spent the first part of his writing life producing reviews, books on nature, and critical studies of writers such as George Borrow and Algernon Charles Swinburne, and turned to poetry, under the influence of Robert Frost, in his mid-thirties. Most of his poetry was written after he had enlisted to fight in the First World War and he is frequently thought of as a War Poet, although most of his poems are focused on nature and the countryside rather than dealing directly with his military experiences. A brief collection, *Six Poems* (1916) was published during his lifetime under the pseudonym Edward Eastaway, but most of his poetry, included in

Poems (1917), appeared after his death in action in April 1917, shortly after arriving at the front.

Oliver St John Gogarty (1878–1957)

Oliver St John Gogarty was a surgeon, poet, author, and noted wit in early Twentieth Century Dublin, and a fellow student at University College of James Joyce, who based the character of Buck Mulligan in his novel *Ulysses* on him. He produced several prose autobiographical memoirs, including *As I Was Going Down Sackville Street* (1937), *Tumbling in the Hay* (1939) and *It Isn't This Time of Year at All* (1954). He wrote three plays and a total of 15 volumes of poetry, many of them mannered, witty, and elegant lyrics and elegies about his Dublin contemporaries. W.B. Yeats included 17 of his poems in his *Oxford Book of Modern Verse* (1936), and much of his work was gathered together in his *Collected Poems* (1951). However, scores of other poems were unpublished until after his death.

W.W. Gibson (1878–1962)

Wilfrid Wilson Gibson was a native of Northumberland, many of whose poems were about the region's landscapes, life and characters, including fisherman, miners, and industrial workers. He was a close friend of Rupert Brooke. He published several volumes of poetry in Northumberland, including *Stonefolds* (1907) and *The Web of Life* (1908), and carried his concern for working people into his war poetry. Although Gibson never served abroad, his collections *Battle* (1915) and *Livelihood* (1917) were highly influential in portraying the experiences of ordinary soldiers. His *Collected Poems 1905–1925* was published in 1926. Later volumes included *The Island Stag* (1947) and *Within Four Walls* (1950).

John Masefield (1878–1967)

John Masefield served as a merchant seaman until abandoning his ship in New York, where he lived for three years as a vagrant and odd job man, and also worked in a carpet factory. Returning to England, he took a job for a while as a journalist and published his first book of poems, *Salt-Water Ballads* (1902), drawing on his experiences at sea. This book included his famous poem *Sea Fever*. Masefield also wrote long narrative poems, including *Dauber* (1913) and *Reynard the Fox* (1919), which focuses on English rural life. His *Collected Poems* was published in 1923 and won considerable popularity, leading to his appointment in 1930 as Poet Laureate, a post he held for 37 years until his death. He also produced several plays, a number of works of autobiography and history, and more than 20 novels for children and adults.

Harold Monro (1879–1932)

Harold Monro was born in Brussels of Scottish parents, and became a respected publisher and critic, who founded the Poetry Bookshop in London, and also the influential magazine *Poetry Review*. He was a close friend of many poets, including Wilfred Owen, and published several books of his own poetry, including *Strange Meetings* (1917) and *Children of Love* (1919). His *Collected Poems* (1933) appeared posthumously, with an introduction by T.S. Eliot.

Alfred Noyes (1880–1958)

Alfred Noyes published his first book of poetry, *The Loom of Years* (1901) while still a student at Oxford University, which he left without taking a degree. Five more volumes of poetry followed over the next five years, and in 1914 he began teaching at Princeton University. Noyes was a passionate opponent of modernist ideas in literature, and his own most famous work – notably the narrative poem *The Highwayman* (1906) – is reminiscent of the great poets of the Victorian era. Noyes published nearly 60 books, including poems, short story collections, and novels. His collection of eight songs, *Pageant of Empire* (1924) was set to music by Sir Edward Elgar.

Padraic Colum (1881–1972)

Padraic Colum was a leading figure in the Irish literary revival of the early Twentieth Century, writing plays for Dublin's Abbey Theatre and helping to found the journal *Irish Review*. His early poems, heavily inspired by rural Irish traditions, myths, and folklore, appeared in Dublin magazines and were collected in his first book, *Wild Earth* (1907). In 1914, he settled in the United States, where he published two volumes of Hawaiian folklore and a number of novels and highly regarded collections of children's stories, along with several more books of poetry, including *Dramatic Legends* (1922) and *Creatures* (1927).

John Drinkwater (1882–1937)

John Drinkwater was working as an insurance clerk in London when his first book, *Lyrical and Other Poems* (1908) was published by Harold Monro's Samurai Press, to be followed three years later by *Poems of Men and Hours* (1911). In 1918, his play *Abraham Lincoln* was performed to an enthusiastic reception to be followed by several other successful dramas, and although he continued to publish poetry, he is now generally thought of as a dramatist rather than a lyric poet. He was a close friend of a number of Georgian poets, including Rupert Brooke, for whom he wrote an elegy, *Rupert Brooke* (1915).

James Joyce (1882–1941)

James Joyce is best known as the author of the monumental 'stream of consciousness' novels *Ulysses* (1922) and *Finnegans Wake* (1939). His first book of poetry *Chamber Music* (1907) – a title which he said referred to the sound of urine hitting the side of a chamber pot – was followed by his famous volume of short stories, *Dubliners* (1914). Another book of verse, *Pomes Penyeach* (1927) also received critical praise, and his *Collected Poems* appeared in 1936 – but Joyce's most powerful, original, poetic, and evocative writing is undoubtedly contained in his novels.

James Stephens (1882–1950)

James Stephens grew up as an orphan in the slums of Dublin, which later provided a setting for many of his fairy tales. After struggling to educate himself through reading, he found employment as a solicitor's clerk, and got to know the writer George William Russell (AE), who encouraged the publication of his first book of poetry, *Insurrections (1909)*. This was followed by his first novel, *The Charwoman's Daughter* and a prose fantasy, *The Crock of Gold* (both 1912), which became a children's classic and made him famous. Apart from several other novels and collections of short stories, and *Insurrection in Dublin* (1916), a classic account of the Easter Uprising in Dublin, Stephens became a noted lyric poet. His poetry collections, many of them about animals, and often inspired by Celtic mythology and history, included *Here Are Ladies* (1913), *Songs From the Clay* (1915), and *Collected Poems* (1926).

A.A. Milne (1882–1956)

Alan Alexander Milne was the son of the head of a small independent school in north London, and was educated at Cambridge University, where he edited the University magazine *Granta*. After graduating, he worked for *Punch* magazine, and wrote 18 well-received plays and three novels before producing the monumentally successful and sentimental poems which make up *When We Were Very Young* (1924) and his children's story book, *Winnie-the-Pooh* in 1926. These were quickly followed by *The House at Pooh Corner* (1928) and another book of poems with a similarly arch humour, *Now We Are Six* (1927), all the books being illustrated by E.H. Shepherd. Milne continued writing until crippled by a stroke in the early 1950s, producing several novels and non-fiction works and a number of plays, including *Toad of Toad Hall* (1929), a stage adaptation of Kenneth Grahame's children's story *The Wind in the Willows*.

T.E. Hulme (1883–1917)

Thomas Ernest Hulme, a leading member of the anti-Romantic Imagist movement in early Twentieth Century literature and a champion of modern abstract art, was born in the English Midlands and educated at Cambridge, from where he was expelled for hooliganism. His phrase 'the hard, dry image' came to exemplify the Imagist writing of such poets as James Joyce, Ezra Pound, and William Carlos Williams. Hulme's poetic influence, cut short by his death in World War I, was much greater than his own meagre output would suggest: his *Complete Poetical Works* (1912), published in the magazine *New Age*, consisted of five poems, to which a sixth was added later. He also translated the works of the French philosophers Henri Bergson and Georges Sorel.

William Carlos Williams (1883–1963)

The American poet William Carlos Williams was a doctor in New Jersey who wrote short stories, plays, critical essays and translations as well as a volume of autobiography, *I Wanted to Write a Poem* (1958), and more than 20 books of poetry, in an influential literary career that spanned more than 50 years. He was an important influence on American poetry of the Twentieth Century and, at least in his early poems, a leading member of the Imagist movement. His first published book was *Poems* (1909), but it was with *Spring and All* (1923), a collection of prose and free verse that included his most famous poem, *The Red Wheelbarrow*, that he came to wide public attention. His most ambitious work, *Paterson* (1946–1958) was a massive poem in five volumes which focused on the relationship between man and the modern industrial city. Williams's late collection, *Pictures from Brueghel and Other Poems* (1962) was awarded a posthumous Pulitzer Prize.

James Elroy Flecker (1884–1915)

James Elroy Flecker, educated at Uppingham public school and Oxford University, followed a career in the British consular service and was influenced throughout his short life by a passion for the east. He died of tuberculosis at the age of 30, but his writings already included five volumes of poetry, starting with *The Bridge of Fire* (1907) and including *The Golden Journey to Samarkand* (1913); two plays, including his famous drama *Hassan* (published posthumously 1922); and two novels. A quotation from *The Golden Journey to Samarkand* appears on the Special Air Service Regiment's memorial in Hereford:

> 'We are the Pilgrims, master; we shall go
> Always a little further; it may be
> Beyond that last blue mountain barred with snow
> Across that angry or that glimmering sea.'

D.H. Lawrence (1885–1930)

David Herbert Lawrence abandoned a teaching career on the success of his first novel, *The White Peacock* (1911) and became one of the most controversial novelists of the Twentieth Century. He was already writing poetry and short stories when *The White Peacock* appeared, and developed a strikingly original form of free verse. Apart from his 13 novels, several volumes of short stories, nine plays, and numerous works of non-fiction, he published nine books of poetry during his lifetime, including *Birds, Beasts, and Flowers* (1923), much of which he worked on while living in Sicily, Ceylon, Australia, and New Mexico. A further three volumes of poetry appeared posthumously.

Andrew Young (1885–1971)

Andrew Young was a minister of the Free Church in Scotland who later moved to Sussex and joined the Church of England. His first book of poetry, *Songs of Night* (1910) was published at his father's expense, and was followed by a number of other slim volumes of verse, and by three different editions during his lifetime of his *Collected Poems* (1936, 1950, 1960). His poetry was generally concerned with religion, nature and botanical subjects.

Ezra Pound (1885–1972)

Ezra Pound, famously honoured in T.S. Eliot's dedication of his poem *The Waste Land* (1922) as '*il miglior fabbro*' (the greater craftsman), was the son of Quaker parents in Idaho. His first volume of poems, *A Lume Spento* (*With Taper Quenched*) (1908), was published at his own expense while he was living in Venice. Moving to London, he published several other volumes of verse, including *Personae* (1909), *Canzoni* (1911), and *Lustra* (1916), and was one of the most important members of the Imagist school of poetry. His wide learning in the ancient and modern literature of both Europe and the East was reflected in the richly allusive *Cantos* (1917–1970), which occupied him for the rest of his life. Support for the Italian dictator Mussolini and wartime broadcasts on Italian radio led to his arrest by US forces in 1945. Charged with treason, he was found unfit to plead and confined in a mental institution until 1958. On his release, he returned to Italy where he died. Pound's greatest work, *Cantos*, is unfinished, fragmentary, and largely formless, but he is now considered to have been one of the most influential figures in modern English literature.

Frances Cornford (1886–1960)

Frances Cornford was born Frances Darwin, a granddaughter of the naturalist Charles Darwin, and was educated privately in Cambridge.

There, she married the distinguished scholar Francis Cornford, and afterwards spent most of her life writing poetry. Her first published book, *Poems* (1910), included her most famous poem, the cruelly comic triolet *To a Fat Lady Seen from a Train*. Much of the rest of her poetry, contained in volumes including *Spring Morning* (1915), *Different Days* (1928), *Mountains and Molehills* (1934), and *Travelling Home* (1948), was similarly short and incisive. Her *Collected Poems* appeared in 1954.

Siegfried Sassoon (1886–1967)

Siegfried Sassoon, educated at public school and Cambridge University – which he left without a degree – lived the privileged life of a young country gentleman and published several volumes of poetry at his own expense, before volunteering for military service in 1914. He was awarded the Military Cross for gallantry, but was increasingly disenchanted with the conduct of the war, and was eventually declared unfit for service. Two volumes of his own war poetry, *The Old Huntsman* (1917) and *Counter-Attack* (1918) failed to catch the public mood, but he was influential in encouraging the young Wilfred Owen to continue writing. He was also a close friend of Robert Graves. After the war, the publication of his *Selected Poems* (1925) and *Satirical Poems* (1926) added to his reputation as a poet, and he also began to write his highly acclaimed fictionalised autobiography in three books, *Memoirs of a Fox-Hunting Man* (1928), *Memoirs of an Infantry Officer* (1930), and *Sherston's Progress* (1936). These were followed later by a three-volume genuine autobiography. Sassoon continued to write poetry, but never recaptured the passion, bitterness, and fire of his earlier work.

Rupert Brooke (1887–1915)

Rupert Brooke had a privileged and glittering youth at Rugby School, where his father was a master, and afterwards at Cambridge University. His first book, *Poems 1911* (1911), followed by the publication of his work in the first two anthologies of *Georgian Poetry* in 1912 and 1915, helped to establish him as one of the most popular young poets of his generation, described by W.B. Yeats as 'the handsomest young man in England'. Publication of his hugely popular war sonnets, *1914* (1915), including the famous *The Soldier* ('If I should die, think only this of me') coincided with news of his death from septicaemia on the Greek island of Skyros, as he travelled to the Dardanelles. Today, his ideas about war seem gauche and naïve, compared with the more realistic, experience-based work of poets such as Wilfred Owen, Siegfried Sassoon, and Isaac Rosenberg. One of the fascinating questions of early Twentieth Century literature is how Brooke might have developed as a poet if he had shared their experiences of combat.

Edwin Muir (1887–1959)

Edwin Muir was born in the Orkney Islands, although his family moved to Scotland when he was 14. Travelling in Europe as a young man, he collaborated with his wife on a series of translations from German, especially of the works of Franz Kafka. He published eight volumes of traditional but visionary and occasional apocalyptic poetry, starting with *First Poems* (1925) and including *The Voyage* (1946) and *The Labyrinth* (1949), the books which established his reputation as a poet. Muir also wrote several important critical works, three novels, and a highly-regarded autobiography.

Edith Sitwell (1887–1964)

Edith Sitwell, the Yorkshire-born sister of the writers Osbert and Sacheverell Sitwell, was an experimental and controversial poet whose collection *Façade* (1922), accompanied by music by William Walton, caused angry demonstrations in the audience. Sitwell continued to work at the collection for 15 years and, together with further volumes of poetry during the twenties, including *Bucolic Comedies* (1923) and *The Sleeping Beauty* (1924), it established her as one of the leading voices of the avant-garde. Sitwell's later poetry was heavily influenced by her conversion to Catholicism in 1955. Her autobiography *Taken Care Of* (1965) was published posthumously.

Marianne Moore (1887–1972)

Marianne Moore was born in St Louis, Missouri, starting her literary career with contributions to the magazine *The Egoist*. Her first publication was *Poems* (1921) which was published in London, followed in New York by *Observations* (1924). She was a friend of both Ezra Pound and T.S. Eliot, who admired her work. Her *Complete Poems*, many of them substantially rewritten since their original publication, appeared in 1967.

T.S. Eliot (1888–1965)

Thomas Stearns Eliot's poem *The Waste Land* (1922) was one of the seminal works of the Modernist movement in English literature, and along with his other poems, including *Ash Wednesday* (1930), the play *Murder in the Cathedral* (1935), and particularly *Four Quartets* (1936–1942), marks him out as a leader of the anti-Romantic movement and one of the most important figures in the revitalisation of English literature in the Twentieth Century.

Eliot, who was an influential literary critic and a successful publisher as well as a poet and playwright, was born in St Louis, Missouri. He studied at Harvard University before travelling to France in 1910 to continue his studies at the Sorbonne and, after returning to Harvard for three more years, was awarded a scholarship to Merton College, Oxford in 1914. Although he only spent a year at Merton, he remained in England as a schoolteacher and then a bank clerk, marrying the ballet-dancer Vivienne Haigh-Wood in 1915 and living for a while with the philosopher Bertrand Russell.

His first collection, *Prufrock and Other Observations* (1917), which contained the famous *Love Song of J. Alfred Prufrock*, caused controversy among critics who were used to Romantic and Georgian poetry, because of its uncompromising language and its bleak view of the world. His next collection, *Poems* (1920), which contained the ground-breaking psychological interior dramatic monologue *Gerontion*, was similarly controversial, although today unease about the poetry centres more on its perceived anti-Semitism than on its literary style. However, the disputes over these early poems were as nothing compared with the furore that greeted the 434 lines of *The Waste Land* (1922) five years later.

Eliot spent several years writing the poem, which was completed while he was being treated in France after a serious nervous breakdown in 1921. He had become friendly with the American poet Ezra Pound in 1914, and Pound was instrumental in stripping the language and structure of *The Waste Land* until some critics declared it was incomprehensible – the discovery of the original manuscripts during the 1960s revealed that

Eliot's original poem was almost twice as long as the published version which Pound had edited. Its perceived difficulty was not helped by Eliot's frequent erudite references and allusions not only to German, Italian, French and English literature, but also to Celtic mythology and eastern philosophy and religion.

But despite the initial shock which it caused, *The Waste Land* established Eliot's international standing as a poet. It has an apparently loose structure, with a series of apparently unrelated incidents and scenes reflecting a world of anxiety and uncertainty which waits in fear and without hope of salvation. Lines from it, such as 'April is the cruellest month' and 'I will show you fear in a handful of dust' have become familiar quotations.

However, Eliot had also been establishing a reputation as a literary critic, with the publication of a book of his essays, *The Sacred Wood* (1920), in which he stressed the importance of working within the enduring tradition of western European literature. These essays are considerably more useful in reaching an understanding of *The Waste Land* than the opaque and self-consciously academic *Notes* which Eliot published to the poem. Rather than the Romantic focus on the poet's own individual responses, Eliot declared that the poet should make 'a continual surrender of himself' and become an integral part of the continuing literary tradition.

In 1922, he founded the quarterly review *Criterion*, which he edited until it ceased production in 1939. Further collections of critical essays were *The Use of Poetry and the Use of Criticism* (1933) and *The Classics and the Man of Letters* (1942).

In 1925, Eliot left Lloyds Bank, where he had been working, to join the publishers Faber and Gwyer, (later Faber and Faber), where he remained for the rest of his life, eventually as a director. Two years later, he became a member of the Church of England, and took British citizenship. Other poems followed expressing his sombre disenchantment with modern life, particularly *The Hollow Men* (1925), *Ash Wednesday* (1930), and *Collected Poems 1909–1935* (1936), which included *Burnt Norton*, the first of four poems which together would represent Eliot's greatest achievement.

Over the next six years, he added three more poems, *East Coker* (1940), *The Dry Salvages* (1941) and *Little Gidding* (1942). They were published together as *Four Quartets* in the US in 1943 and in Great Britain the following year, presenting a deeply religious and mystical meditation on humanity in relation to time, tradition, history and eternity.

While developing *Four Quartets*, Eliot had also been working on a series of verse dramas which occupied him until 1958. *Burnt Norton* had been inspired by one of these, his treatment of the story of Thomas à Becket in *Murder in the Cathedral* (1935), and this was followed by four more, *The Family Reunion* (1939), *The Cocktail Party* (1949), *The Confidential Clerk* (1953) and *The Elder Statesman* (1958). He had also produced the collection of light verse, *Old Possum's Book of Practical Cats* (1939) which was later adapted for the stage as the musical *Cats*.

In 1948, recognised both nationally and internationally as one of the most profound literary voices of his day, he was appointed to the Order of Merit and awarded the Nobel Prize for Literature.

Eliot was formally separated in 1932 from his first wife, who was admitted to a mental hospital six years later, and remained there until her death in 1947. In 1957 he married his secretary, Valerie Fletcher, and lived happily with her until his death in London at the age of 76 from emphysema. His ashes were buried at East Coker, the Somerset village from which his ancestors had emigrated to America, and which he had immortalised in *Four Quartets*.

Julian Grenfell (1888–1915)

Julian Grenfell, the Eton and Oxford-educated son and heir of Lord Desborough, joined the army in 1910 and wrote in a letter home soon after the start of World War I, 'I adore war.' He compared it to a picnic. The following year, as an officer in the Royal Dragoons, he was killed at Ypres. His best-known poem, *Into Battle*, a mystical glorification of the nobility of the fighting man, was published on the day of his death.

John Crowe Ransom (1888–1974)

John Crowe Ransom was born in Tennessee, the son of a Methodist minister. After service as an artillery officer in World War I, he followed a career as a university teacher, and founded the influential *Kenyon Review* while working at Kenyon College in Ohio. His first book of poetry, *Poems About God* (1919) attracted critical praise, but *Chills and Fever* (1924) and *Two Gentlemen in Bonds* (1927) are generally seen as his most successful work. Ransom also achieved an international reputation as a literary critic, particularly with his books *God Without Thunder* (1930) and *The New Criticism* (1941).

Isaac Rosenberg (1890–1918)

After studying at the Slade School of Art, Isaac Rosenberg joined the army in 1915, against the wishes of his pacifist family, largely to escape the poverty of his life in London. He never shared the early enthusiasm for combat of other war poets, and from the start his poetry sought to present the reader with the physical realities of combat from the point of view of the individual soldier. He was killed in battle in April 1918. Rosenberg's pre-war poetry in *Night and Day* (1912) and *Youth* (1915) was largely ignored, although admired by both T.S. Eliot and Ezra Pound, but his so-called 'trench poems', notably *Break of Day in the Trenches* and *Louse Hunting*, led to his gradual acceptance as one of the most original of the war poets.

A.P. Herbert (1890–1971)

Sir Alan Patrick Herbert was a Member of Parliament and an active legal campaigner on issues such as divorce law reform, but he is remembered most as a witty and original humorist. He was a longstanding contributor of essays and poems to *Punch*, the author of several comic operas, including *La Vie Parisienne* (1929) and *Bless the Bride* (1947), and also creator of over a hundred *Misleading Cases* (1927–1966), a series of comic stories highlighting absurdities in the British legal system. His collected light verse was published in *A Book of Ballads* (1949).

Vita Sackville-West (1892–1962)

Vita (Victoria) Sackville-West, the author of 17 novels, including *All Passion Spent* (1931), was born into an aristocratic family in Kent, where she spent most of her life. She started writing poetry as a child, and produced several books of verse, starting with *A Dancing Elf* (1912), and including her most famous poem, *The Land* (1927), which describes the changes to the Kentish countryside through the seasons. Her *Collected Poems* appeared in 1933. She was married to the diplomat and writer Harold Nicholson, but scandalised contemporary society with a series of

passionate homosexual affairs, her many lovers including the novelist
Virginia Woolf.

Sir Osbert Sitwell (1892–1969)

Sir Osbert Sitwell, younger brother of Dame Edith Sitwell, began writing
poetry as a soldier in World War I, and later produced several books
of poems, including *The Collected Satires and Poems* (1931), *Mrs Kimber*
(1937), and *Wrack at Tidesend* (1952). He also wrote novels, short stories,
and criticism, and a series of well-received volumes of autobiography.

Hugh MacDiarmid (Christopher Murray Grieve) (1892–1978)

Christopher Murray Grieve, who wrote under the pseudonym Hugh
MacDiarmid, worked as a journalist and editor after World War I,
producing anthologies of contemporary Scottish writing. His own first
books of poetry, *Sangschaw* (1925) and *Penny Wheep* (1926), began the
process of bringing the Scots language of Robert Burns back into modern
Scottish literature. These were followed by *The Drunk Man Looks at the
Thistle* (1926), a lengthy dramatic monologue of over 2,500 lines, which
established him as the leading figure in what became known as the Scottish
literary renaissance. He wrote several other books in both Scots and
Standard English, including several translations from Scottish Gaelic
and two volumes of autobiography, *Lucky Poet* (1943) and *The Company
I've Kept* (1966).

Wilfred Owen (1893–1918)

The reputation of Wilfred Edward Salter Owen rests upon a single volume
of poems, mostly written over a period of just over 12 months between
August 1917 and September 1918, and unpublished for two years after his
death. He is now generally acknowledged as the most important of the
small group of First World War Poets who revealed the truth about
the horrors of trench warfare to an outraged public.

Owen was born in Oswestry, Shropshire, but the family had to move to
lodgings in the town of Birkenhead when he was four years old, on the
death of his grandfather. His family's poverty meant that he was unable to

take up a place at London University, and shortly before the outbreak of World War I he was employed as a private tutor in English and French in Bordeaux, where he worked on a planned collection of poems, to be called *Minor Poems – in Minor Keys – by a Minor*.

The book, perhaps fortunately, was never published: Owen volunteered for the Artists' Rifles in 1915, and was commissioned as a second lieutenant in the Manchester Regiment in 1916 and drafted to France early the following year. His early poems are self-conscious, sub-Keatsian, and entirely conventional Georgian verses about throstles and bees, 'merry England' and 'gay fairyland', which gave no hint of any conspicuous literary talent. Although his experience of conflict was limited to four months, with only five weeks of that spent in battle on the front line, the intensity of the suffering he saw and experienced transformed him and his poetry completely.

Owen arrived at Beaumont Hamel on the Somme in January 1917, during the worst winter of the war, and after an intensive spell of combat which included several days sheltering from heavy fire in a shell hole close to the dismembered body of another soldier he was diagnosed with shell shock and invalided out to Craiglockhart Military Hospital, near Edinburgh. While he was there, he was encouraged by his doctor to start writing poetry again as therapy, and edited *The Hydra*, a magazine produced by and for the inmates. Later he met the established poet and outspoken critic of the war Siegfried Sassoon, who introduced him to Robert Graves, read and commented on his writing, and advised him to concentrate on the experiences he had endured at the Front.

The following January, having read about a mining disaster in Staffordshire, he wrote *Miners*, which relates the suffering of the coal-miners to that of soldiers in the trenches. It appeared in *The Nation*, one of only five poems to be published during his lifetime. Returning to France as a company commander after spending more than a year in hospital and under treatment, he took part in the successful assault on the Hindenberg Line at Joncourt in October 1918, where he was awarded the Military Cross for 'conspicuous gallantry'.

Under Sassoon's influence, however, Owen had begun to question the justice of the war, and letters home demonstrate that he did not expect to survive this second tour of front-line duty – one sent to his mother contained a quote from the Indian writer Rabindranath Tagore, 'When I go from here, let this be my parting word, that what I have seen is unsurpassable.' Another letter told her: 'I have suffered seventh hell. I have not been at the front. I have been in front of it. I held an advanced post, that is, a dugout in the middle of No Man's Land ...' He was determined to continue to tell the story of the suffering of the front-line soldiers through his poetry.

Owen was killed by German machine-gun fire on November 4 1918, just a week before the end of the fighting, during an operation to cross the Sambre-Oise canal at Ors. News of his death reportedly reached his family in Oswestry as church bells were ringing in the town to celebrate the coming of peace. He was buried alongside his military comrades in a cemetery at Ors, near where he fell.

Encouraged by Sassoon, Owen had begun to arrange the poems he had written at Craiglockhart and afterwards ready for publication, and had written his famous unfinished preface, in which he declared: 'Above all, this book is not concerned with Poetry. The subject is war and the pity of War. The Poetry is in the pity.'

Owen was angered by the jingoistic and sentimental writing of non-combatants who had glorified the war – an early plan was to write a sarcastic dedication of his own collection to the rabble-rousing versifier Jessie Pope, who had written about the war as 'the red crashing game of a fight'. However, his poems were remarkable not just for the shocking immediacy of their impact, in such graphic pieces as *Dulce et Decorum Est*, but also for their technical mastery and innovation. Owen was the first modern poet systematically to employ pararhyme, the technique of using words with the same consonants but different vowel sounds, like hall/hell or grained/ground. In many of his poems, such as *Strange Meeting*, this innovation produces a haunting atmosphere of dislocation and uneasiness.

The preface was found by Siegfried Sassoon when he was sorting through the various drafts and different versions of Owen's poems after his death, and used in the edition which he published in December 1920. Another compilation with a memoir about Owen and his poetry was made by Edmund Blunden (1931), but Owen's popularity grew only slowly – as late as 1937, he was omitted from W.B. Yeats's *Oxford Book of Modern Verse*. By that time, however, many critics saw Yeats's decision as perverse, and Owen gradually came to be seen as one of the most important spokesmen for a lost generation. In 1962, his poems were chosen by Benjamin Britten to be set alongside the Latin Requiem Mass in his *War Requiem*, and a fresh *Collected Poems*, edited by Cecil Day-Lewis, appeared the following year. Today, Owen's role in creating a new form of war poetry, based on realism, direct personal experience and occasionally brutal honesty, is firmly established.

Richard Church (1893–1972)

Richard Church began writing poetry as a young man, while working as a civil servant in the Department of Customs and Excise, and published several books of verse, including *The Flood of Life* (1917) and *The Glance Backward* (1930). He left the civil service in 1933 to become a full-time writer, producing more books of wistful Georgian poetry, a number of novels for both adults and children, and three volumes of autobiography.

E.E. Cummings (1894–1962)

The Harvard-educated American poet Edward Estlin Cummings caused controversy with the experimental and eccentric typography, grammar, punctuation, and phrasing of the poems in his first collection, *Tulips and Chimneys* (1923). It is not certain that he preferred the non-capitalised version of his name generally used today, but Cummings continued to experiment in his subsequent 11 books of poetry, which included *&* (1925), consisting of poems cut out of the earlier book by the publisher; *is 5* (1926); and *No Thanks* (1935), which he published privately and dedicated to the 14 publishers who had turned it down. However, the challenging and avant-garde appearance of his work may sometimes distract attention from its meaning: Cummings wrote strikingly erotic love poetry, bitter satires about contemporary life, and powerful appreciations of the individual soul. He also produced a prose account of his imprisonment in a French detention camp in World War I, *The Enormous Room* (1921); an account of a journey in Russia, *Eimi* (1933); and *Tom* (1935), a ballet loosely based on Harriet Beecher Stowe's novel *Uncle Tom's Cabin*.

Robert Graves (1895–1985)

Robert Graves was educated at Charterhouse School and, after being seriously wounded in World War I, Oxford University. By the time he went to Oxford, he had already published three books of war poetry, *Over the Brazier* and *Goliath and David* (both 1916) and *Fairies and Fusiliers*

(1917). His later autobiographical prose account of the conflict, *Goodbye to All That* (1929), became a classic, as did his novels *I, Claudius* (1934) and *Claudius the God* (1935). Graves published more than 40 collections of love poems, ballads, songs, dramatic monologues, and narrative verse, along with translations and interpretations such as *The Greek Myths* (1935) and *The Hebrew Myths* (1963, with Raphael Patai), as well as several other novels and biographies and a historical and mystical study of the nature of poetry, *The White Goddess* (1948). By the time he died at the age of 90, he had published more than 140 books. He enjoyed a 13-year relationship with the American poet Laura Riding, who is often credited as the inspiration for much of his work.

Edmund Blunden (1896–1974)

Edmund Blunden grew up in Kent, and images from the Kentish countryside recurred in his poetry throughout his life. He taught English literature in the universities of Tokyo, Hong Kong, and Oxford, and also spent several years as a literary journalist. He served in the trenches in World War I, but although his prose memoir, *Undertones of War* (1928) is highly regarded, his war poems are overshadowed by the poetry of rural life which he wrote in the years after the war, in such books as *The Waggoner* (1920), *The Shepherd* (1922) and *English Poems* (1925). However, the experience of combat, often treated calmly and contemplatively, remained a major theme in collections like *After the Bombing* (1950), published while Blunden was teaching in Tokyo. Apart from his own prolific work, Blunden contributed to English literature by promoting the forgotten poetry of John Clare, and producing an important collected edition of the poems of Wilfred Owen.

Hart Crane (1899–1932)

Hart Crane, the son of a successful Ohio businessman, published two books of poetry during his lifetime, *White Buildings* (1926) and *The Bridge* (1930), which uses Brooklyn Bridge as a symbolic starting point for a consideration of the historic, literary, and mythological roots of America. Other poems were published in magazines and his *Collected Poems* appeared in 1938. Crane's poems are notoriously oblique and difficult – a characteristic which some critics ascribe to the need in his day to avoid acknowledging his homosexuality. A chronic alcoholic for much of his adult life, he committed suicide at the age of 32.

Sir Noel Coward (1899–1973)

The wit, poet, and dramatist Noel Coward (the son of a piano salesman) appeared professionally on the stage from the age of 12. He is best known for his frequently-quoted witticisms and for the massively successful musicals, operettas, reviews and comedies of manners, such as *Hay Fever* (1925) and *Blithe Spirit* (1941), which he wrote in a career spanning more than 50 years. In the theatre, he was universally known as The Master. His output included more than three hundred songs, such as *Mad Dogs and Englishmen* from *Words and Music* (1932), and the satiric *Don't let's Be Beastly to the Germans* (1943). Coward, who was knighted in 1970, also produced three books of light verse, *Chelsea Buns* (1925), *Spangled Unicorn* (1932) and *Not Yet the Dodo* (1967). His *Collected Verse* appeared in 1984, 11 years after his death.

Jorge Luis Borges (1899–1986)

The Argentinian writer Jorge Luis Borges spent much of his youth in Europe, returning to Argentina in his early twenties to publish his first collection of poetry, *Fervor de Buenos Aires* (*Fervour of Buenos Aires*) (1923). This was followed by many other books of poetry, essays, short stories, translations, and criticism, published all over the world. His collections of poetry include *El Otro, el Mismo* (*The other, the same*) (1969), *La Rosa Profunda* (*The Deep Rose*) (1975), and *Historia de la Noche* (*History of the Night*) (1979). Borges became blind in his late fifties due to a hereditary condition, and died in Geneva, Switzerland.

Roy Campbell (1901–1957)

The South African poet Ignatius Royston Dunnachie Cambell – Roy Campbell – was a fascist sympathiser in the 1930s who supported Franco in the Spanish Civil War and drew on his experiences in a long poem, *Flowering Rifle* (1939) which caused controversy because of its perceived militarism and fascist sympathies. However, he served in World War II in Africa. His first poem, *The Flaming Terrapin* (1924), was an allegory about Creation, but after coming to England in 1927, he began to publish bitter satires about the writers of the Bloomsbury Group, notably *The Georgiad* (1931), a long poem in heroic couplets. He also wrote lyrical poetry, which was published in several collections, including *Adamastor* (1930), *Flowering Reeds* (1933), *Mithraic Emblems* (1936), and *Talking Bronco* (1936). Campbell's work was highly praised by fellow poets including T.S. Eliot and Dylan Thomas. His other writings included several translations from Spanish, French, and Portuguese, and two highly regarded if variably reliable volumes of autobiography.

Laura Riding (1901–1991)

Laura Riding was one of several pseudonyms adopted by Laura Reichenthal (later Laura Gottschalk and Laura Jackson), who was born in New York and began to write poetry while studying at Cornell University, New York State. Her first poem was published in the influential poetry magazine *The Fugitive* (1923), and her first book of poetry, *The Close Chaplet* (1926) – strikingly original, and written in free verse – followed three years later. Riding's association with Robert Graves led to the joint publication of *A Survey of Modernist Poetry* (1927), a seminal work of literary criticism which dismissed much contemporary poetry except for their own work and that of e.e. cummings. She wrote about 20 books of poetry, criticism, and stories, although she renounced poetry shortly after the publication of her *Collected Poems* in 1938.

Michael Roberts (1902–1948)

Michael Roberts was a physics and mathematics teacher whose first book of poetry appeared in 1930. Christened William Edward Roberts, he adopted the name Michael in honour of his hero, the Russian poet and scientist Mikhail Lomonosov. He was close to W.H. Auden, and is best known as a critic and anthologist responsible for the collection *New Country* (1933), which featured Auden's work, and for *The Faber Book of Modern Verse* (1933).

Stevie Smith (1902–1971)

Stevie Smith was born in Yorkshire, and christened Florence Margaret Smith – the 'Stevie' was a nickname that simply stuck. She worked as a private secretary, and published her first book of poetry, *A Good Time Was Had By All* (1937) just a year after the appearance of the first of her three novels, *Novel on Yellow Paper* (1936). Two more novels followed, and seven other books of verse, frequently blending serious themes such as death or failed love with a witty, often enigmatic fervour. Her most famous poem, *Not Waving But Drowning*, appeared in a collection of the same name, published in 1957. She illustrated her own books, and was famous for presenting her verse in well-attended and popular readings. Her letters, prose writings, and previously uncollected poetry were published posthumously in *Me Again: Uncollected Writings of Stevie Smith, Illustrated by Herself* (1984).

Patrick Kavanagh (1904–1967)

The Irish poet Patrick Kavanagh grew up on a farm in County Monaghan before leaving for London and then Dublin, where he worked as a journalist, in his mid-twenties. His first volume of poems, *The Ploughman and Other Poems* (1936), established his lasting interest in rural Irish life. His best-known poem, *The Great Hunger* (1942) is a long satirical narrative work of biting social realism which introduces the Irish farmer Patrick Maguire as a symbol of the poverty and despair of the countryside. Kavanagh's later books included *A Soul for Sale* (1947) and *Come Dance with Kitty Stobling* (1960). He also wrote several novels and three works of autobiography. His *Collected Poems* appeared in 1964 and *Collected Prose* three years later.

C. Day Lewis (1904–1972)

Cecil Day Lewis was born in Ireland, the son of a clergyman, but was brought up in England and educated at public school and Oxford University. His first book of poetry, *Beechen Vigil* (1925) appeared while he was still a student. At Oxford, he became part of a left-wing group of poets led by W.H. Auden, a friendship which influenced his own work, and which lasted through the 1930s. His poetry during this period, notably in his verse sequence *The Magnetic Mountain* (1933) and in volumes such as *Collected Poems 1929–1933* (1935) was overwhelmingly concerned with his political beliefs. In later collections, particularly *Word Over All* (1943) and *Pegasus and Other Poems (1957)* , he moved away from political verse towards a more traditional lyricism. His translations of Virgil's *Georgics* (1940), *Aeneid* (1952), and *Eclogues* (1963) were very highly praised. Early in his career, Day Lewis worked as a teacher, and later supplemented his earnings by writing successful detective novels under the pseudonym Nicholas Blake. He was appointed Poet Laureate in 1968, following the death of John Masefield.

Norman Cameron (1905–1953)

Norman Cameron was born in India of Scottish parents, and educated in Edinburgh and at Oxford University, later working in advertising. He was a friend of Robert Graves, Laura Riding, Dylan Thomas, and W.H. Auden, but his own small output of poetry, appearing in magazines and journals in the 1930s and then in *The Winter House* (1935) was highly distinctive. Two further volumes of poems followed, generally brief, succinct, and built around a single powerful image – *Work in Hand* (1942, a collaboration with Robert Graves and the poetry publisher Alan Hodge) and *Forgive Me, Sire* (1950). He also translated the French poetry of François Villon, Honoré de Balzac, and Arthur Rimbaud. Cameron's posthumous *Collected Poems 1905–1953* appeared in 1957.

Idris Davies (1905–1953)

Idris Davies, the son of a Welsh miner, worked as a miner himself and then qualified as a teacher. His first collection of poems, *Gwalia Deserta* (1938) was in Welsh, but later he wrote in English. His poems were often angry, and dealt mainly with working class life and class struggle, and included *The Angry Summer, a Poem of 1926* (1943), about the General Strike, and *Tonypandy and Other Poems* (1945). T.S. Eliot, who was a great admirer of his work, edited his *Selected Poems* (1953), and his *Collected Poems* appeared posthumously in 1972.

Geoffrey Grigson (1905–1985)

Geoffrey Grigson, who earned a reputation as an outspoken and trenchant literary critic and essayist, was born in the Cornish village of Pelynt, the son of a vicar. He edited the influential literary magazine *New Verse*, and also several poetry anthologies, including *The Faber Book of Popular Verse* (1971). His own volumes of poetry, starting with *Several Observations* (1939) and including *The Isles of Scilly* (1946), *Angles and Circles* (1974) and *History of Him* (1980), were largely set in Cornwall, and were known for the detail and precision of their observation. Grigson also wrote critical studies of several writers and artists, including John Clare and Wyndham Lewis, as well as an autobiography, *The Crest on the Silver* (1950).

Vernon Watkins (1906–1967)

Vernon Watkins was born of Welsh-speaking parents in Maesteg, Glamorgan, and went to Cambridge University, which he left after one year. He worked as a bank clerk and later a teacher in the Swansea area, where he became close to Dylan Thomas. During World War II, he worked at the secret code-breaking centre at Bletchley Park. *The Ballad of the Mari Lwyd*, the title poem of his first collection (1941), draws heavily on Welsh mythology, and much of his later work was also strongly inspired by the life and traditions of his native country. He published a total of seven books of poetry during his lifetime, including *The Lady with the Unicorn* (1948), *The North Sea* (translations from Heine, 1951), and *Affinities* (1962). Three more collections appeared after his death.

Sir John Betjeman (1906–1984)

John Betjeman, the son of a prosperous furniture manufacturer, was educated at Marlborough School and Oxford, before working briefly as a schoolmaster and then as an architectural journalist. His first collection, *Mount Zion* (1931) was followed by several others, including *Old Lights for New Chancels* (1940) and *New Bats in Old Belfries* (1945), which quickly won him widespread popularity. His *Collected Poems* first appeared in 1958. Apart from his many well-known poems of middle-class life, such as *In Westminster Abbey* (1940) and *How to Get on in Society* (1958) – in which Betjeman demonstrates his acute observation and sensitive ear for snobbish affectation, coupled with a sharp satirical edge – he also wrote *Summoned By Bells* (1960), a blank verse autobiography, and more than 40 books, mainly of architectural criticism. He also became a favourite television broadcaster, and was Poet Laureate from 1972 until his death.

Sir William Empson (1906–1984)

William Empson was educated at Winchester College and Cambridge University, from where he was expelled after contraceptives were found in his room. He is best-known for his ground-breaking critical study of English poetry, *Seven Types of Ambiguity* (1930), and other critical works such as *Some Versions of Pastoral* (1935) and *The Structure of Complex Words* (1951). His own poetry, published in *Poems* (1935) and *The Gathering Storm* (1940), is frequently complex and analytical, with abstruse references to modern physics and mathematics – qualities that have led to comparisons with John Donne, whom he greatly admired. Empson wrote very little poetry after 1940. His *Collected Poems* was first published in 1949, and he was knighted in 1979.

Samuel Beckett (1906–1989)

The Nobel Prizewinning dramatist, author, and poet Samuel Beckett was born in a suburb of Dublin and educated at Trinity College before becoming a teacher in Belfast and Paris. During World War II, he fought with the French Resistance in Paris before escaping to the unoccupied zone of France in 1942. Beckett had already produced a number of stories and two volumes of poetry, *Whoroscope* (1930) and *Echo's Bones* (1935), but his most creative period came in the years immediately following the War. Writing in both French and English, he produced some of his best-known prose narratives including *Molloy* (pub 1951) and *Malone Dies* (pub 1951) and two plays, including *En Attendant Godot* (pub 1952), the French version of *Waiting for Godot* (pub 1955). It was several years before he could find publishers for any of these works. Among his other best-known dramatic works are *Endgame* (1957), *Krapp's Last Tape* (1958), *Happy Days* (1960), and *Not I* (1972). He had been publishing poetry in both French and English magazines and periodicals, and his *Collected Poems in English* (1961) was followed 16 years later by *Collected Poems in English and French* (1977). Like many of his plays, his last poem, *What is*

The Poets

the Word (1988), written shortly before his death, dealt with the difficulty of communication through spoken words. Beckett was awarded the Nobel Prize for Literature in 1969.

Christopher Caudwell (Christopher St John Sprigg) (1907–1937)

Christopher St John Sprigg chose his mother's maiden name, Caudwell, as a pseudonym for his astonishingly wide-ranging literary work, none of which appeared in his lifetime. He was the son of a journalist, and worked as a reporter himself before joining the Communist Party and travelling to Spain to fight in the Civil War. He was killed there at the age of 29 on his first day in battle, shortly before the publication of his first book, *Illusion and Reality* (1937), a study of poetry from a Marxist and sociological viewpoint. Other books followed, including novels, short stories, and works of sociology, science, and technology. *Poems* (1939), brought together some of his poetic writings, among them *Hymn to Philosophy*, which sought to put poetry and philosophy into a historical context, *The Progress of Poetry*, and *Classic Encounter*. Caudwell's *Collected Poems* appeared in 1986, nearly 50 years after his death.

Louis MacNeice (1907–1963)

Louis MacNeice was born in Belfast, but educated at Marlborough College and Oxford University where he met the poet W.H. Auden. Together with Stephen Spender and Cecil Day Lewis, they became known as the leading 'Thirties Poets' and were derisively dubbed MacSpaunday by Roy Campbell. MacNeice dismissed his first book, *Blind Fireworks* (1929) as juvenilia, but it was followed by more than a dozen other collections, which established him as a technically masterful and strikingly original poet in his own right. *Autumn Journal* (1939) is his best-known poem, charting the ominous approach of World War II against a backdrop of conflict in Spain. Apart from other collections such as *Ten Burnt Offerings* (1952) and *Visitations* (1957), MacNeice wrote a number of successful plays, two novels, several works of literary criticism, translations from Latin and Greek, a book of autobiography, and *Letters from Iceland* (1937, with W.H. Auden).

111

W.H. Auden (1907–1973)

Wystan Hugh Auden, the son of a highly respected physician and professor of public health, was born in York into a strongly Anglo-Catholic Christian family, and educated at public school and Christ Church College, Oxford. Even before he reached university, he had published his first poem in a collection entitled *Public School Verse* (1924), and during his time at Oxford he formed lasting friendships with other poets, including the future Poet Laureate Cecil Day Lewis, Louis MacNeice, and Stephen Spender. The group later became known as the Thirties Poets or the Pylon Poets, a reference to the frequent use of industrial imagery in their poems.

After Oxford, Auden spent a year in Berlin, where he fell in love with the German language and German literature, but also first experienced the atmosphere of political menace that became a central theme of his poetry. He also spent time there with his future collaborator as a playwright, the novelist Christopher Isherwood, whom he had known at school, and with whom he enjoyed a sporadic homosexual relationship for several years.

Returning to England in 1929, he worked as a private tutor and school-teacher, publishing his first collection of poetry, *Poems* (1930) the following year. (An earlier collection, also entitled *Poems*, was printed privately in a limited edition of fewer than 50 copies by Stephen Spender in 1928). These pieces, mixing references to the Icelandic sagas, Anglo-Saxon poetry, left wing politics, and psychoanalysis, set the tone for much of Auden's early work and established his reputation as an important new voice.

Auden, who had developed the habit of asking Isherwood's advice on his poems before they were published, followed this volume with *The Orators* (1932), a verse and prose study, and *Look, Stranger!* (1936), a collection of 31 poems. This latter book was dedicated to Erika Mann, the lesbian daughter of the German novelist Thomas Mann, whom Auden married in 1936 to enable her to escape from Nazi Germany with a British passport.

He was also writing plays, in collaboration with Isherwood, including *The Dog beneath the Skin* (1935), *The Ascent of F6* (1937) and *On the Frontier* (1938). He also produced two well-received travel books around this time, *Letters from Iceland* (1937), with MacNeice, which chronicled a trip they made to Iceland during 1936, and *Journey to a War* (1939) with Isherwood, recording their impressions in prose and verse of a six-month visit to the Sino-Japanese war.

From 1935, he worked with the composer Benjamin Britten in the Film Unit of the GPO, the state post office. Among the pieces they produced for the GP was the short film *Night Mail* (1936), featuring Auden's much-anthologised poem and Britten's original musical setting. He also spent two months in 1937 observing the Spanish Civil War in support of the Republican cause, although he later suggested that the poem he produced as a result of his journey, *Spain* (1937) marked the start of his disillusionment with left wing politics.

At the time, however, he remained an iconic figure among political left-wingers warning against the rise of totalitarianism in Europe, although he later confessed, 'I know that all the verse I wrote, all the positions I took in the thirties, didn't save a single Jew.'

His trip to China with Isherwood had taken him through the United States and they returned there to live early in 1939. Shortly afterwards, he met the teenage American poet Chester Kallman, with whom he settled down in a long-term relationship, becoming, in Alan Bennett's phrase, 'an early GI bride'. Starting in the 1950s, Auden and Kallman collaborated on several libretti for music by Hans Werner Henze, Nicolas Nabokov, and other composers.

Auden's decision to live in New York just as war was approaching in Europe – he stayed there throughout the war, and became an American citizen in 1946 – damaged his standing at home, especially when his collection *Another Time* (1940) included his poem dealing with the individual response to political evil, *September 1 1939*. Several of the well-known poems in the collection, including *Musée des Beaux Arts*, were written before the move to America, but others include Auden's elegy to the poet W.B. Yeats, *In Memory of W.B. Yeats*, his satirical *The Unknown Citizen*, and *In Memory of Sigmund Freud*.

Further collections followed, many with religious themes as Auden approached again the Christian faith that he had lost as a young man, among them *The Double Man* (1941) published in Britain as *New Year Letter*; and *For the Time Being* (1944). *The Age of Anxiety* (1947), a long dramatic poem which starts in a New York bar in night-time and seeks to set religious and philosophical uncertainty in an industrialised world, was awarded a Pulitzer Prize in 1948. The publication of the *Collected Poetry of W.H. Auden* (1945) provided an opportunity to review a long and varied career, and also to revise several of his earlier poems.

Auden published a total of more than four hundred poems, ranging from traditional ballads to Japanese haiku. He habitually rewrote earlier poems for new collections, and occasionally rejected some that he considered to have been dishonest. Among the latter group was his famous *September 1 1939*.

In the post-war years, he began spending his summers in Europe, notably on the Italian island of Ischia, which featured in his poem *In Praise of Limestone*, which appeared in his collection *Nones* (1951). He also began writing literary criticism, publishing *The Enchafèd Flood* (1950) and *The Dyer's Hand* (1962), a collection of his lectures as Oxford University Professor of Poetry, a post to which he was appointed for five years in 1956.

During his Professorship, he spent only a few weeks in Oxford each year, giving his lectures and returning to New York in the winter and Italy and Austria during the summer. In 1972, however, he finally left New York to spend his winters at his old college, Christ Church, in Oxford. He died in Vienna in 1973, and was buried in the churchyard in the small town of Kirchstetten, where he had a summer home.

John Lehmann (1907–1987)

John Lehmann, younger brother of the novelist Rosamond Lehmann, was educated at Eton and Cambridge University. He is best remembered today as an influential journalist, editor and publisher, who founded the journals *New Writing* and *The London Magazine*. Apart from several collections of his own poems, starting with *A Garden Revisited* (1931) and three volumes of autobiography, *The Whispering Gallery* (1955), *I Am My Brother* (1960) and *The Ample Proposition* (1966), Lehmann also wrote biographies of Rupert Brooke, Edith Sitwell, and Virginia Woolf.

Kathleen Raine (1908–2003)

Kathleen Raine, who developed a lifelong fascination for mystical and visionary philosophy while at Cambridge University, was a poet, critic, and scholar who wrote 11 separate collections of lyrical and contemplative poetry, beginning with *Stone and Flower* (1943), and including *The Pythoness*

(1949), *The Hollow Hill* (1965), *The Lost Country* (1971) and *Living With Mystery* (1972). She also wrote three volumes of autobiography, and a number of critical studies, particularly of William Blake and W.B. Yeats.

Malcolm Lowry (1909–1957)

The novelist Malcolm Lowry, best known for *Under the Volcano* (1947), started a life of travelling by signing on as a deckhand on a merchant ship to China before going up to Cambridge University. Later in his life he lived at various times in France, New York, California, Mexico and Canada. A chronic alcoholic, he published little during his lifetime, but *Selected Poems of Malcolm Lowry* (1962) appeared posthumously, along with a collection of short stories and several other prose works.

James Reeves (John Morris) (1909–1978)

James Reeves was the pseudonym of John Morris, who was educated at Stowe School and Cambridge University before becoming a teacher. His first book of poetry, *A Natural Need* (1936) was followed by several other collections, both for children and adults, including *The Wandering Moon* (1950), *The Talking Skull* (1958), and *The Closed Door* (1977). Reeves was most noted for his children's verse, and also for his work on collecting and interpreting traditional poetry and songs.

Stephen Spender (1909–1995)

Stephen Spender is generally thought of as one of the group known as the Thirties Poets, centred on W.H. Auden and also including Louis MacNeice and Cecil Day-Lewis, even though he was not particularly close to any of them. Spender's early poetry was self-consciously political – particularly *Poems* (1933), his long poem *Vienna* (1934) on social unrest in Austria, and his verse play *Trial of a Judge* (1938) – and he joined the International Brigades fighting in the Spanish Civil War. He continued to write poetry all his life, his last book of verse, *Dolphins* (1994) appearing when he was 85 years old, but he became better known after the war as a critic, editor of *Encounter* magazine and one of the founders of *Index on Censorship*. Spender was knighted in 1983.

Norman MacCaig (1910–1996)

The Scottish poet Norman MacCaig spent many years as a schoolmaster, later becoming Reader in Poetry at the University of Stirling. In his later life, he dismissed his two first books, *Far Cry* (1943) and *The Inward Eye* (1946) as needlessly obscure: it was not until the publication of *Riding Lights* (1955) that he began to demonstrate his distinctive sharp wit, flashes of wry humour, and imaginative metaphors. Several other collections followed, including *The Sinai Sort* (1957), *Measures* (1965), *Rings on a Tree* (1968) and *A Man in My Position* (1969). MacCaig is now considered one of the most important Scottish poets of the Twentieth Century, and the best of his work is sometimes compared, maybe flatteringly, with that of John Donne.

Lawrence Durrell (1912–1990)

Lawrence Durrell was born in India, coming to England at the age of 11. Now remembered primarily as a novelist, particularly for his *Alexandria Quartet* (1957–1960), he was also a prolific author of travel books, plays, and poetry. His first short collection of poems, *Quaint Fragments* (1931), was followed by seven more books of poetry, including *A Private Country* (1943) and *On Seeming to Presume* (1948). Durrell travelled widely throughout his life, living at various times in Corfu, France, Egypt, Argentina, and Serbia (former Yugoslavia), and writing about many of these places in his highly regarded travel books. He was the brother of Gerald Durrell, the famous conservationist and writer.

Roy Fuller (1912–1991)

Roy Fuller wrote more than 40 novels and books of poetry while pursuing a full-time career as a solicitor. His first book, *Poems* (1939), seemed to be heavily influenced by W.H. Auden, but he rapidly developed his own distinctively calm and measured tone, with its flashes of icy satire. The collections which followed, such as *The Middle of a War* (1942), *Buff* (1965), and *Available for Dreams* (1989) presented a lucid but reflective view of day to day life, and an increasing ironic fascination with the challenges of old age. Fuller was Professor of Poetry at Oxford University from 1968 to 1973. Apart from his poetry and novels for both adults and children, he published two collections of his Oxford lectures and four volumes of memoirs.

R.S. Thomas (1913–2000)

Ronald Stuart Thomas was an Anglican clergyman whose collections of poems, starting with *The Stones of the Field* (1946), expressed his passionate devotion to Wales, its landscape, and its people. Although he wrote his poetry in English, he remained a dedicated nationalist, who frequently drew attention to the poverty of rural Wales in lines that could be bitterly critical of the people themselves and what he saw as their cultural decay. Among his poetry collections were *Poetry for Supper* (1958), *Frequencies* (1978), *Between Here and Now* (1981) and *Later Poems 1972–1982* (1983). Thomas also produced a volume of autobiographical essays in Welsh, *Neb* (*No One*) (1985), and edited *The Penguin Book of Religious Verse* (1963) and selections of the poetry of Edward Thomas, George Herbert, and William Wordsworth.

Dylan Thomas (1914–1953)

Dylan Thomas, probably the most popular Welsh poet of the Twentieth Century, began his writing career as a junior reporter on the *South Wales Evening Post*. He was 20 years old when his first book of poetry, *18 Poems* (1934) was published to considerable acclaim; he had just moved to London. Other collections followed, but it was with *Deaths and Entrances* (1946), which contained Thomas's famous poem about his Welsh child-hood, *Fern Hill*, that he began to reach a wider audience. By this time, his drinking had become a serious problem, but his reputation as a reader of his own work began to grow rapidly, and more collections followed, among them *In Country Sleep* (1952), which includes the much-quoted villanelle addressed to his dying father, *Do Not Go Gentle Into That Good Night*. He was also writing for the BBC, and in 1953 delivered the radio play *Under Milk Wood*, his magical evocation of the imaginary town of Llareggub – a name which, it was rapidly noted, spells 'Bugger all' backwards. The play was broadcast in January the following year, but by that time Thomas was dead, having collapsed while on a visit to New York.

Henry Reed (1914–1986)

The poet Henry Reed, who served in World War II as a Japanese translator and went on to write radio plays for the BBC, is best known for a single poem, the deceptively languid *Naming of Parts*. The poem, described by the poet Vernon Scannell as 'probably the most widely quoted and anthologised single poem written in the Second World War', is the first of a series of six named *Lessons of the War*, which was published in the *New Statesman* magazine in 1942 and included in Reed's collection *A Map of Verona* (1946). His parody of T.S. Eliot's *Four Quartets*, *Chard Whitlow*, is included in the same book. Reed also published two collections of his radio plays, *The Streets of Pompeii* (1971) and *Hilda Tablet and Others* (1971).

Laurie Lee (1914–1997)

Laurie Lee, best known today for his evocative and nostalgic auto-biographical memoirs *Cider with Rosie* (1959) and *As I Walked Out One Midsummer Morning* (1969), began his adult life as an office worker before embarking on travels across Europe in the mid 1930s. He was also an accomplished poet: his three collections, *The Sun My Monument* (1944), *The Bloom of Candles* (1947) and *My Many-Coated Man* (1955), demonstrate the same sensuous fascination with nature and rural life that he later showed in *Cider With Rosie*. Lee also wrote a number of film scripts for the Ministry of Information and the BBC before and after the war, a volume of short stories, *I Can't Stay Long* (1976), and a third volume of autobiography, *A Moment of War* (1991).

Alun Lewis (1915–1944)

Alun Lewis grew up in a South Wales mining village and worked as a schoolteacher before joining the army, despite his committed pacifism, shortly after the outbreak of World War II. His first collection, *Raiders' Dawn* (1942) deals mainly with his experiences in training camps in England, and includes his famous poem *All Day It Has Rained*. Lewis published a collection of short stories, *The Last Inspection* in the same year. He was sent to fight in the Far Eastern campaign, and died in Burma. His second book of poetry, *Ha! Ha! Among the Trumpets*, (1945) appeared posthumously.

G.S. Fraser (1915–1980)

The Scottish poet, literary critic and teacher George Sutherland Fraser worked as a literary journalist in London in the 1940s after returning from war service in the Middle East and Africa. Apart from his collections of poems, which included *The Fatal Landscape* (1941), and *The Traveller Has Regrets* (1948) he edited a number of anthologies, including collections of the poetry of John Keats and Keith Douglas, and wrote several studies of poets and writers, as well as his *Short History of English Poetry* (1981) Fraser spent the last 20 years of his life as an academic and teacher at the University of Leicester.

Gavin Ewart (1916–1995)

Although Gavin Ewart's first published poem appeared when he was 17 years old, and his first collection, *Poems and Songs* (1939) when he was 33, he spent many years as an advertising copywriter before becoming a full-time writer in his mid-fifties. His second volume, *Londoners* (1964) was the first of many more books of poetry which was light and comic, but often with an acid satiric bite. He also had a talent for erotic verse, which shocked some people and made some of his books, such as *Pleasures of the Flesh* (1966), briefly controversial. Among his other collections were *Or Where a Young Penguin Lies Screaming* (1977), *All My Little Ones* (1978) and *More Little Ones* (1982). Ewart also edited several anthologies, including *The Penguin Book of Light Verse* (1980). The poet Philip Larkin marked Ewart's sixty-fifth birthday with a poem comparing reading his verse to enjoying a nightly glass of malt whisky.

Charles Causley (1917–2003)

The Cornish poet Charles Causley wrote several of the poems that comprised his first collection, *Farewell, Aggie Weston* (1951) while serving in the Royal Navy during World War II. By this time he was working as a teacher in Cornwall, and he continued to publish regular books of direct and deceptively simple poetry for both children and adults – without always making the distinction – for the next 30 years. These included *Survivor's Leave* (1953), *Union Street* (1957), *Underneath the Water* (1968), and *Secret Destinations* (1984). Many of his poems showed the influence of the popular music tradition, possibly from his time playing piano in a dance band in his youth.

Robert Conquest (1917–)

Robert Conquest was born in Worcestershire to a Norwegian mother and an American father, and has held senior academic posts in both Britain and the US. He is well known as one of the world's most distinguished Soviet historians and the author of more than 20 books on the Soviet Union, in particular his account of Stalin's purges, *The Great Terror* (1968). However, he is also a very prolific writer of light verse and strikingly erotic love poetry. In 1956, he edited the influential anthology *New Lines*, which included the poetry of Philip Larkin, Thom Gunn, and Kingsley Amis, as well as his own work. Among the collections of his own poetry Conquest has published are *Poems* (1955), *Between Mars and Venus* (1962), *Forays* (1979), and *Penultimata* (2009).

John Heath-Stubbs (1918–2006)

John Francis Alexander Heath-Stubbs was afflicted from childhood with progressive blindness, and although he did not lose his sight completely until his was 59 years old, even as a young man he had to hold the page a couple of inches from his eyes in order to read. He spent some time teaching, both in schools and universities. His poetry, from his first public collection, *Wounded Thammuz* (1942) was traditional, classical, and heavily allusive. Other books included *Beauty and the Beast* (1943), *The Swarming of the Bees* (1948), and *Artorius* (1972), an epic poem based on the legend of King Arthur, as well as translations of the fourteenth century Persian poet Hafiz and the Nineteenth Century Italian Romantic poet Giacomo Leopardi.

James Kirkup (1918–2009)

James Falconer Kirkup was the only son of a carpenter in South Shields, Co. Durham. He published around 40 collections of poetry, starting with *The Drowned Sailor* (1947), and including *Prodigal Son – Poems 1956–1959* (1959), *White Shadows, Black Shadows* (1970), and *Throwback* (2004). He also wrote six books of autobiography and a number of translations of novels from French and German writers. His controversial poem *The Love That Dares to Speak Its Name* (1976), in which a Roman centurion speaks about having sex with the dead body of Christ, led to the successful prosecution for blasphemy of *Gay News*, the magazine that printed the poem, and its editor, Denis Lemon. Kirkup, who spent 30 years as Professor of English at Japan's Kyoto University, was also known for his mastery of the Japanese haiku and tanka forms, both in translation from the original and in his own poetry.

Keith Douglas (1920–1944)

Keith Castellain Douglas, the son of a former soldier turned failed chicken-farmer, was already recognised as one of his generation's most promising poets when he was a student at Oxford University, but he left the university early to join the army soon after the outbreak of war. By 1941, he was serving as a tank commander in North Africa, where he wrote some of his best poems and completed the memoir later published as *Alamein to Zem-Zem* (1946). He was brought back to England for the D-Day invasion, and was killed in battle in Normandy at the age of 24. Douglas's *Selected Poems* (1943) appeared while he was still in North Africa, but it was the detached observation mixed with an insightful and passionate sympathy of poems like *Vergissmeinnicht* and *Simplify Me When I'm Dead*, published in his posthumous *Collected Poems* (1951), that established him as one of the most significant voices of World War II.

D.J. Enright (1920–2002)

Dennis Joseph Enright spent much of his career as an English teacher in universities in the Far East, and much of his poetry is marked by its eastern settings and its fascination with the contrast between western and eastern cultures. Apart from over a dozen books of poetry, starting with *The Laughing Hyena and Other Poems* (1953) and including *Bread Rather Than Blossoms* (1956), *Addictions* (1962), *Foreign Devils* (1972) and a sequence of poems developing the Faust legend, *A Faust Book* (1979), Enright wrote several critical studies of poetry and literature and a number of novels for children.

John Gillespie Magee (1922–1941)

John Gillespie Magee, who died at the age of 19 in an accident while a pilot in the Royal Canadian Air Force, is known for a single poem, *High Flight*, sent home in a letter to his parents shortly before his death. Phrases from the poem were used by US President Ronald Reagan in his tribute to the astronauts who died in the Challenger disaster in 2003, when he said they had 'waved goodbye and slipped the surly bonds of earth to touch the face of God.' Magee, the son of an American father and a British mother, died in a mid-air collision during a training flight over Lincolnshire. His poem features in many anthologies and was included in *The Complete Works of John Magee: the Pilot Poet* (1989).

Philip Larkin (1922–1985)

Philip Larkin, the famously reclusive librarian of Hull University, summed up the popular view of his poetry with the quip 'Depression is to me as daffodils were to Wordsworth'. His first collection, *The North Ship* (1944) appeared soon after he left Oxford University, and was followed by a novel, *Jill* (1946). Further poetry collections, *The Less Deceived* (1955), *The Whitsun Weddings* (1964), and *High Windows* (1974), included such famous poems as *Church Going*, *An Arundel Tomb*, and the much-quoted *This Be the Verse*. Larkin is noted for his fear of death, particularly in his later poem *Aubade* (1977), but his poetry also shows a gentle nostalgia, a sense of the fragility of culture and civilisation, and a wry loneliness. Larkin also wrote many articles on jazz, one of his passions, and edited *The Oxford Book of Twentieth Century English Verse* (1973).

Kingsley Amis (1922–1995)

London-born Kingsley Amis, a lifelong friend and Oxford contemporary of the poet Philip Larkin, achieved international fame with his deceptively subversive novel *Lucky Jim* (1954). By that time he had already produced three volumes of poetry, *Bright November* (1947), *A Frame of Mind* (1953) and *Fantasy Portraits* (1954), and he continued to write poetry intermittently throughout his career as a novelist and essayist. Like his novels, his poems were generally straightforward, but often with a subtle and nuanced subtext. Amis also became well known as an anthologist, particularly for his *New Oxford Book of Light Verse* (1978).

Donald Davie (1922–1995)

Donald Davie was born in Barnsley, Yorkshire, and educated at Cambridge University, where he later taught. He also held academic posts at various times at Trinity College, Dublin, Essex University, and Stanford University, California. His poetry, beginning with his collection *Brides of Reason* (1955), has been described as austere and elegant, often tackling complex philosophical themes. Other collections included *A Winter Talent* (1957), entitled *Essex Poems* (1969), and *In the Stopping Train* (1977). Critical works included *Purity of Diction in English Verse* (1952), a study of Ezra Pound entitled *Poet as Sculptor* (1964), and a study of contemporary English poetry, *Under Briggflatts: a History of Poetry in Great Britain 1960–1988* (1989).

Alan Ross (1922–2001)

Alan Ross, editor of the well-regarded *London Magazine* for 40 years, was born in India, and allegedly spoke better Hindustani than English when he came to school in England at the age of eight. He was a journalist and cricket enthusiast who wrote several books on the game. Ross's first poetry collection *The Derelict Day* (1946) contained a number of poems written while he was serving in the Royal Navy during World War II, and was followed by several other collections, including *Poems 1942–1967* (1967) and *Death Valley* (1980). Apart from his poems and his works on cricket and cricketers, Ross also wrote a number of travel books, two volumes of autobiography, and a well-reviewed study of war artists, *The Colour of War* (1983).

Vernon Scannell (1922–2007)

Vernon Scannell, sometime soldier, fairground boxer, and teacher, wrote poetry for both children and adults, novels, and autobiography. His collection *Walking Wounded* (1965), published 20 years after the end of World War II, has led to his being considered one of the leading poets of the war. His first volume, *Graves and Resurrections* (1948), which he later dismissed as 'woolly and wordy', was followed by several novels and more books of verse, including *A Mortal Pitch* (1957), *A Sense of Danger* (1962) and *The Apple Raid* (1974). He completed his final collection, *Last Post* (2007) shortly before his death.

Dannie Abse (1923–)

Dannie Abse, who was born in Cardiff, qualified as a doctor and practised as a specialist at a chest clinic for over 30 years. His first collection of poetry, *After Every Green Thing* (1949) has been followed by over 50 volumes of poetry, novels, autobiography, memoir, and anthologies. His poetry collections include *Way Out in the Centre* (1981), *Ask the Bloody Horse* (1986), and *White Coat, Purple Coat: Collected Poems 1948–1988* (1989). His memoir *The Presence* (2007) is a moving tribute to his wife, the art historian Joan Mercer, who was killed in a car accident in 2005. Abse's *New Selected Poems* was published in 2009.

David Holbrook (1923–)

After war service which included participation in the D-Day landings of 1944 – the inspiration of his novel *Flesh Wounds* (1966) – David Holbrook followed a career as a teacher and academic, becoming a full-time writer in the mid 1960s. His first book of verse, *Imaginings* (1960), was followed by five other new collections and his *Selected Poems 1961–1978* (1980). Holbrook, a lifelong socialist whose poetry concentrates on the emotional impact of everyday occurrences, has also written extensively on literature, education, philosophy, and social commentary. He is a Fellow of King's College, Cambridge.

John Wain (1925–1994)

The poet, novelist, and critic John Wain spent most of his career as a full-time journalist and author, although he also taught at Reading University and Gresham College London. He was Professor of Poetry at Oxford University from 1973–1978. Apart from his 10 collections of verse, from *Mixed Feelings* (1951) to *Open Country* (1987), Wain wrote 14 novels, several plays and short stories, a volume of autobiography, *Sprightly Running* (1962), and a large number of essays and full-length critical books on various literary subjects, including a biography of Samuel Johnson and a study of the novels of Arnold Bennett.

Christopher Logue (1926–)

Christopher Logue, who was born in Portsmouth, is a poet, playwright, journalist and actor whose major work has been his still-unfinished adaptation of Homer's *Iliad* into modern and idiomatic language, begun in 1959. *War Music* (1981), a collection of the first three instalments of the work, was awarded the Griffin Poetry Prize, while another instalment, *Cold Calls* (2005) won the Whitbread Poetry Award. Much of the poetry in his other collections, starting with *Wand and Quadrant* (1953), is heavily influenced by jazz, and has been performed to a musical accompaniment. Logue has also edited several books of verse for children, written several screenplays and produced an English version of Pablo Neruda's poetry in *The Man Who Told His Love* (1958).

Thom Gunn (1929–2004)

Thom Gunn, the son of a journalist, was born in London, but spent much of his life in the US, teaching at Stanford University and at the University of California. His first two volumes of poetry, *Fighting Terms* (1954) and *The Sense of Movement* (1957) were enthusiastically received by critics, and his poems became more experimental, often concentrating on the themes of homosexuality and drugs. His award-winning *The Man With Night Sweats* (1992) dealt with the AIDS epidemic, in which he lost many friends. *Boss Cupid* (2000) was a collection of poems which were sometimes tragic but often funny and ironic about the random and unpredictable nature of love.

Jon Silkin (1930–1997)

Jon Silkin, the son of a London solicitor, worked as a manual labourer and caretaker for six years, later taking a job teaching English to foreign students while he established himself as a poet and writer. His first published poems appeared in a short pamphlet, *The Portrait and Other Poems* (1950), to be followed by his first book, *The Peaceable Kingdom* (1954). Other collections, including *Nature With Man* (1965), *Amana*

Grass (1971) and *The Principle of Water* (1974) followed at regular intervals. Silkin was also a noted editor and anthologist, responsible for the authoritative *Wilfred Owen: The War Poems* (1994) and *Poetry of the Committed Individual* (1973), which consisted of verse from the literary magazine *Stand*, which he founded in 1952 and edited for more than 40 years.

Ted Hughes (1930–1998)

Edward James Hughes was born in Mytholmroyd, West Yorkshire, and studied at Cambridge University, where he met his future wife, the American poet Sylvia Plath. His first collection, *Hawk in the Rain* (1957) was enthusiastically received by critics. It was followed by another collection, *Lupercal* (1960) and *Selected Poems* (1962, with Thom Gunn), but three years later, Plath killed herself shortly after the couple had parted. Hughes stopped writing for some time after her suicide, but his next book, *Wodwo* (1967) marked the start of an intensely creative period which lasted for the rest of his life. He published several more collections of his characteristically physical, unsentimental, and direct poems, many of them focused on the natural world. These included *Crow* (1970) and *Wolfwatching* (1989). Hughes, who was appointed Poet Laureate in 1984, also edited a number of anthologies, and wrote eight translations and adaptations of classical, French and Spanish originals, notably Seneca's *Oedipus* (1968) and *Tales from Ovid* (1997); and several prose works for both adults and children, including *The Iron Man* (1968). His final collection of poetry, Birthday Letters (1998) explored his troubled relationship with Sylvia Plath.

Anthony Thwaite (1930–)

Anthony Thwaite, poet, broadcaster, critic and academic, was born in Chester and spent much of his early childhood in Yorkshire before being evacuated to the United States during World War II. He is an acknowledged expert on Japanese poetry, and was visiting lecturer at Tokyo University between 1955 and 1957. He co-edited *The Penguin Book of Japanese Verse* (1964, revised 1998). As a journalist, he has worked as a BBC producer, as co-editor of *Encounter* magazine, and as literary editor for the *Listener* and *New Statesman*. Among his own collections of poetry are *Home Truths* (1957), *The Stones of Emptiness, Poems 1963–66* (1967), *Victorian Voices* (1980), *Selected Poems 1956–1996* (1997) and *A Different Country: New Poems* (2000). He is a literary executor of Philip Larkin, and has edited Larkin's *Collected Poems* (1988). Thwaite's *Collected Poems* appeared in 2007.

Derek Walcott (1930–)

The West Indian poet Derek Walcott, winner of the 1992 Nobel Prize for Literature, began his career as a teacher in his native St Lucia, later moving to Boston, Massachusetts, where he taught poetry and drama at Boston University. He has published more than 20 books of poetry, and a similar number of plays, most of them dealing with the life and culture of the West Indies. His collection *In a Green Night: Poems 1948–1960* (1962) established his international reputation with its lush, sensuous evocation of the Caribbean, while later books such as *Sea Grapes* (1976) concentrated on contemporary tensions between European and native West Indian culture. *Another Life* (1973) studied similar themes in a long autobiographical poem, and another book-length poem, *Omeros* (1990) reinterpreted the stories of the *Iliad* and the *Odyssey* from a Caribbean perspective.

Alan Brownjohn (1931–)

Oxford University-educated Alan Brownjohn established his reputation as a poet and writer with several books, starting with his first collection of verse, *Travellers Alone* (1954), written while he was working as a schoolteacher and then a lecturer. He became a full-time writer in 1979, since when he has continued to produce new books of poetry, novels, and collections of verse, including three anthologies for schools. His own collections include *Nineteen Poems* (1980), *The Observation Car* (1990), *The Men Around Her Bed* (2004) and *Collected Poems* (2006). *Philip Larkin* (1975), a critical study of Larkin's poetry, was published in 1975.

P.J. Kavanagh (1931–)

Patrick Kavanagh – known as P.J. Kavanagh to distinguish him from the Irish poet who died in 1967 – once considered becoming a monk, but instead has served as a soldier, fighting in the Korean War, and been an actor, journalist, broadcaster, and lecturer, as well as a full-time writer for some 50 years. His 10 books of poetry, including *About Time* (1970), a single poem in 10 parts dealing with the themes of permanence and continuity in a changing world, *Presences* (1987), *An Enchantment* (1991), and *Something About* (2004), often focus on religion and the natural world. Kavanagh, a prolific writer in magazines and journals, has also produced six novels and a highly regarded biographical memoir, *A Perfect Stranger* (1966), and edited a number of anthologies, including *The Essential G.K. Chesterton* (1985) and *The Oxford Book of Short Poems* (1985). He lives in Gloucestershire.

Sylvia Plath (1932–1963)

Sylvia Plath was born in the United States, and came to Britain on a Fulbright scholarship to study at Cambridge University, where she met the poet Ted Hughes. She already suffered from severe bouts of depression and had made at least one suicide attempt, and after a short and difficult marriage to Hughes, spent in the US and Britain, she killed herself in February 1963. Only one book of poetry, *Colossus* (1960) was published during her lifetime, but the posthumous publication of *Ariel* (1965), a collection of poems mainly written during the bout of depression that preceded her suicide, drew international attention to the deeply personal and confessional nature of her work. Plath also wrote four children's novels and a semi-autobiographical novel for adults, *The Bell Jar* (1963). Two other volumes of poetry, *Crossing the Water* (1971) and *Winter Trees* (1972) were also published posthumously, along with her *Collected Poems* (1981) and several volumes of letters and journals.

George MacBeth (1932–1992)

George MacBeth, the son of a miner, was born in Scotland but brought up and educated in England, where he went to Oxford University. He spent 20 years as a producer, mainly of poetry programmes, for the BBC, leaving the Corporation in 1976 to concentrate on writing novels, including *The Samurai* (1976), *Anna's Book* (1983) and the posthumous *The Testament of Spencer* (1992). He also edited several anthologies, including *The Penguin Book of Animal Verse* (1965) and *The Penguin Book of Victorian*

Verse (1969). MacBeth's early poetry, in volumes such as *A Form of Words* (1954) and *A War Quartet* (1969) often concentrated on dark subjects such as violence, sex, and death, but his later work, including *The Long Darkness* (1983) and *Trespassing: Poems from Ireland* (1991) was generally simpler and more contemplative. His last book, *The Patient* (1992) dealt with the motor neurone disease that finally killed him.

Adrian Henri (1932–2000)

The poet, painter, and sometime rock and roll performer Adrian Henri was born in Birkenhead and spent his life in Liverpool and the north-west of England. Along with Brian Patten and Roger McGough, he was known as one of the 'Liverpool Poets' of the 1960s who led a revival of performance poetry. Apart from appearing in several anthologies of Liverpool poetry, he produced a number of collections of his own, including *Tonight at Noon* (1968), *City* (1969), *From the Loveless Motel* (1980) and *Not Fade Away* (1994). Henri also wrote children's books, and plays for both the stage and television.

Adrian Mitchell (1932–2008)

Adrian Mitchell, born in London and educated at Oxford University, was a leading figure in the Underground poetry movement of the 1970s and 80s, writing strikingly original and frequently angry poems of pacifism and social protest. His collections included *Out Loud* (1969), *Ride the Nightmare* (1971), and *Tell Me Lies: Poems 2005–2008*. The title poem of that last collection, one of his most famous, was first written about the Vietnam War in 1964, and updated over the years to take account of later conflicts. Mitchell also wrote several novels, plays, and television dramas.

Jenny Joseph (1932–)

Jenny Joseph was born in Birmingham and educated at Oxford University before working as a journalist, a teacher and lecturer, and a pub landlady. After winning awards with her first two collections, *The Unlooked-for Season* (1960) and *Rose in the Afternoon* (1974), she published her *Selected Poems* in 1992. Her other work has included prose fiction such as *Extended*

Similes (1997) and combined prose and poetry, in *Persephone* (1986). Jenny Joseph, who lives in Gloucestershire, also writes books for children.

Edward Lucie-Smith (1933–)

Edward Lucie-Smith was born in Jamaica and educated in England before joining the Royal Air Force and subsequently working as an advertising copywriter. He became a full-time writer in the mid-sixties, and has written more than a hundred books of art criticism, history, and biography, as well as editing several anthologies, including *The Penguin Book of Elizabethan Verse* (1965) and *The Penguin Book of Satirical Verse* (1967). His poetry collections include *A Tropical Childhood and Other Poems* (1961), *Silence* (1967), and *Changing Shape* (2002).

John Fuller (1937–)

John Fuller, the son of the poet Roy Fuller, was born at Ashford in Kent, and educated at Oxford University, later working as a university teacher in New York, Manchester, and Oxford. His first poetry collection, *Fairground Music* (1961), was followed by a number of other books of verse, including *Cannibals and Missionaries* (1972), *Lies and Secrets* (1979), *The Illusionists* (1980), and *Song and Dance* (2008). He has also written novels for both children and adults, and edited several anthologies, including *The Chatto Book of Love Poetry* (1990) and *The Oxford Book of Sonnets* (2000).

Tony Harrison (1937–)

The Leeds-born poet, dramatist, and translator Tony Harrison writes passionately about the clash between his northern, working class background and his literary and classical education. This theme of social division is worked out most famously in his poem *V* (for 'versus', in a pun with 'verses'), the perceived obscenity of which caused angry and ill-informed complaints in Parliament when it was filmed for television in 1987. His best-known collections are *The Loiners* (1970) and *The School of Eloquence* (1978). Harrison is also highly regarded as a dramatist, writing films and plays such as *Prometheus* (1998) and *Fram* (2008), which often link classical legends and historical events with the contemporary world.

Roger McGough (1937–)

Along with Brian Patten and Adrian Henri, Liverpool-born Roger McGough first came to fame as one of the Liverpool Poets of the 1960s, and was a member of the comedy pop and poetry group Scaffold for 10 years. He has produced over 40 books of poetry for both adults and children, starting with *Summer with Monika* (1967) and including *Crocodile Puddles* (1984), *Bad, Bad Cats* (1997) and *That Awkward Age* (2009). His *Collected Poems* appeared in 2003. McGough's poetry is notable for its zany humour, truculent politics, and frequent flashes of pathos and simple affection, but he has also written a number of plays, including a translation of Moliere's *The Hypochondriac* (2009). His autobiography, *Said and Done*, was published in 2005

Allan Ahlberg (1938–)

Allan Ahlberg worked as a primary school teacher for 10 years, before starting to write children's books in the 1970s. These were illustrated by his wife Janet Ahlberg, who died in 1994. They were one of the most successful teams in the history of children's writing, producing more than 30 books which sold millions of copies in more than 20 languages. Among their biggest successes were *Burglar Bill* (1977) and *The Jolly Postman* (1986). Allan Ahlberg's two successful poetry collections, *Please Mrs Butler* (1984) and *Heard It In the Playground* (1989) take an irreverent and even subversive look at school life from the viewpoints of both children and teachers.

Seamus Heaney (1939–)

The Irish poet Seamus Heaney, the son of a Northern Ireland farmer, studied at The Queen's University, Belfast, and worked as a schoolteacher and later a university lecturer. His first major collection, *Death of a Naturalist* (1966), won several awards and was followed by other books of poetry, including *Field Work* (1979), *Station Island* (1984), and *The Spirit Level* (1996), which made him one of the best-selling contemporary poets in the English language. Heaney's poetry evokes traditional Irish rural life and history, but links them with contemporary issues such as the violence in Northern Ireland, with a tight focus on individual characters and revelatory moments. He has also written a number of essays on poets, poetry, and language, some of which appeared in two collections of his prose writing, *Preoccupations 1968–1978* (1980) and *Finders Keepers 1971–2001* (2002), and several translations and adaptations from the classics, Irish, and Anglo-Saxon. Heaney won the Nobel Prize for Literature in 1995.

Joseph Brodsky (1940–1996)

The Russian-born Jewish writer Joseph Brodsky moved to the United States in 1972 after serving eighteen months internal exile in Siberia. He worked as an academic and teacher in several universities in the US and Britain, and produced a number of volumes of poetry and essays, starting with *Elegy for John Donne and Other Poems* (1967) and including *Poems* (1972), *Nativity Poems* (2001), and *Collected Poems in English 1972–1999* (2000). Brodsky was awarded the Nobel Prize for Literature in 1987, and appointed Poet Laureate of the United States in 1991.

Bob Dylan (Robert Allen Zimmerman) (1941–)

The American singer-songwriter Bob Dylan, born Robert Allen Zimmerman, was born in Minnesota in the American Midwest, and was involved in folk music from his early youth, signing his first record deal at the age of 20 and changing his name to Bob Dylan the following year, in homage to the poet Dylan Thomas. His most famous early songs included *A Hard Rain's a-Gonna Fall* (1962) and *Blowin' in the Wind* (1963). There have been several printed versions of his songs, including *Lyrics: 1962–2001* (2004), and his poetry collection *Tarantula* appeared in 1966. Although Dylan has facetiously described himself as a 'song and dance man', the critic Christopher Ricks has famously compared him with the Romantic poet John Keats.

Kit Wright (1944–)

Kit Wright, who has written more than 25 books of poetry for both adults and children, was greatly influenced by the poet Vernon Scannell, whom he met as a boy of 17. He had been writing poetry since he was six years old, and continued through Oxford University, while working as a teacher, and during three years working in Canada. Publication of his first collection for adults, *The Bear Looked Over the Mountain* (1974) led a year later to his decision to make his living as a freelance writer. His first children's collection, *Arthur's Father* (1978) followed three years as Creative Writing Fellow at Trinity College, Cambridge. His other collections include *Rabbiting On and Other Poems* (1978), *Cat Among the Pigeons* (1987) and *Hoping It Might be So: Poems 1974–2000* (2000). He has also published several anthologies.

Wendy Cope (1945–)

Oxford University-educated Wendy Cope worked as a primary school teacher before the publication of her first collection, *Making Cocoa for Kingsley Amis* (1986), which was so successful that she became a full-time writer. Other collections of her deceptively simple verse, often focused with irony and a wry understatement on the loneliness of human relationships, have included *Serious Concerns* (1992), *If I Don't Know* (2001), and *Two Cures for Love: Selected Poems 1979–2006* (2008). Cope's parodies of poets such as Sir Philip Sidney and T.S. Eliot, in everyday modern language and with a characteristic concluding bump of bathos, are particularly popular.

Brian Patten (1946–)

After making his name as one of the Liverpool Poets alongside Adrian Henri and Roger McGough in their joint anthology *The Mersey Sound* (1967), Brian Patten published his own first collection, *Little Johnny's Confession*, in the same year. This was followed by a series of books of poetry, including *Vanishing Trick* (1976), *Love Poems* (1981), and *Armada* (1996). Patten is particularly known for his poetry for children, in such books as *Gargling With Jelly: a Collection of Poems* (1985), *The Blue and Green Ark – An Alphabet for Planet Earth* (1999) and *Juggling with Gerbils* (2000). He has also edited a number of poetry anthologies, and published books of prose fiction for both adults and children, most notably *The Story Giant* (2001).

Pam Ayres (1947–)

Pam Ayres was born and brought up in Berkshire and served for several years in the Women's Royal Air Force before being launched into a career as a writer and performer of comic verse by victory in the television talent competition *Opportunity Knocks* in 1975. Her first collection, *Some of Me Poetry* (1976) appeared the following year, to be followed by further books of self-deprecating and ironic verse at regular intervals, including *Thoughts of a Late-Night Knitter* (1978) and *Surgically Enhanced* (2006). Pam Ayres has given live performances of her poetry, with her distinctive regional accent, in the United Kingdom, Australia, and New Zealand, and is a regular contributor to a range of radio programmes.

Grace Nichols (1950–)

Grace Nichols spent her early life in the Caribbean island of Guyana, where she worked as a teacher and a journalist before moving to live in the United Kingdom in 1977. Her first poetry collection, *I Is a Long Memoried Woman* (1983), which drew heavily on her West Indies experiences, was praised by critics and adapted for film and radio. It has been followed by other books of verse, including *Lazy Thoughts of a Lazy Woman* (1989), *Sunris* (1996), and *Picasso, I Want my Face Back* (2009), and by several collections of short stories and poetry for children, such as *Come on into My Tropical Garden* (1988) and *Give Yourself a Hug* (1994).

Sir Andrew Motion (1952–)

Andrew Motion, educated at public school and Oxford University, was Poet Laureate from 1999 to 2009, after the death of Ted Hughes. He won the Newdigate Prize for poetry at Oxford with his poem *Inland*, which was later included in his collection, *The Pleasure Steamers* (1977). Subsequent collections have included *Secret Narratives* (1983), *Dangerous Play: Poems 1974–1984* (1984), *Selected Poems 1976–1997* (1998) and *The Cinder Path* (2009). Motion has also written several highly acclaimed biographies, most notably lives of John Keats and Philip Larkin, and a short novel, *The Invention of Dr Cake* (2003). *Ways of Life: On Places, Painters and Poets* (2008) is a selection of his autobiographical and critical writings.

Carol Ann Duffy (1955–)

Carol Ann Duffy, appointed Poet Laureate in 2009, in succession to Andrew Motion, was born in Glasgow but brought up in the English West Midlands. She is not only Britain's first woman Laureate, but also the first openly bisexual poet to hold the post. She lived for several years with the poet Adrian Henri in Liverpool. After graduating from Liverpool University with a degree in philosophy, she worked as a literary journalist and lecturer for some years while continuing to write and read her poetry. Among her collections of poetry – 'comprised of simple words used in a complicated way', as she put it – are *Standing Female Nude* (1985), *Mean Time* (1993), *Feminine Gospels* (2002) and *Rapture* (2005). She has also written several collections for children, including *Meeting Midnight* (1999) and *The Hat* (2007), as well as producing a number of picture books. Her plays, including *Take My Husband* (1982) and *Little Women, Big Boys* (1986) have been performed in Liverpool and London, and she has also edited several anthologies of poetry. Duffy's poems, frequently studied in schools, are praised as accessible, entertaining and funny, but often have a bitter, incisive edge.

Benjamin Zephaniah (1958–)

The poet, novelist and playwright Benjamin Zephaniah was born in Birmingham, and grew up there and in Jamaica. His first poetry collection, *Pen Rhythm* (1980) has been followed by several others, including *The Dread Affair* (1985), and *Funky Chickens* (1996), all of which he says aim to interest people who do not read books. His collection *The Little Book of Vegan Poems* (2001) marks his commitment to veganism and animal rights, while *Too Black, Too Strong* (2001) was the product of his time as poet-in-residence at the London chambers of the radical barrister Michael Mansfield. Zephaniah has also written a number of novels, plays, and books for children, and has released several music recordings, including *Us and Dem* (1990) and *Belly of de Beast* (1996).

Simon Armitage (1963–)

Simon Armitage worked for six years as a probation officer before establishing himself as a professional writer and poet with the success of his first collection, *Zoom!* (1989). Other books of his poems, which are set firmly in contemporary life and often written with a wry or even black humour, include *Kid* (1992), *The Dead Sea Poems* (1995), *The Shout: Selected Poems* (2005), and *Out of the Blue* (2008). Armitage, who lives in West Yorkshire, has also produced highly praised translations of Homer's *Odyssey* (2006) and *Sir Gawain and the Green Knight* (2007), written two novels, and edited several poetry anthologies, including a selection of poems by Ted Hughes. He writes for radio, television, and film, and has is the author of four plays.

Glossary

A

Allegory
A poem such as Spenser's *Faerie Queene*, in which individual characters carry a specific moral or symbolic meaning.

Alliteration
The effect achieved when words starting with the same letter are used together, such as Wordsworth's 'dances with the daffodils' (*The Daffodils*) or 'And sings a solitary song, that whistles in the wind' (*Lucy Gray*). Anglo-Saxon and Middle English poetry was often built around alliteration.

Antistrophe
The second stanza of a Pindaric ode, which follows and enlarges upon the strophe.

Assonance
The effect achieved by using words which do not rhyme, but have a similar vowel sound, like Wilfred Owen's 'Down some profound dull tunnel, long since scooped' (*Strange Meeting*).

Augustan
Poetry of the Eighteenth Century such as that of Pope, Dryden, and Swift, based on the style and philosophy of Virgil, Horace, and Ovid and other Latin poets of the time of the Emperor Augustus.

Avant-garde
French expression, translated as 'vanguard', referring to experimental and innovative artistic or literary work.

B

Ballad
A narrative poem often written in imitation of traditional poetry which was passed down by word of mouth. Ballads, such as Coleridge's *Rime of the Ancient Mariner*, frequently rhyme ABCB:

> 'It is an ancient mariner
> And he stoppeth one of three.
> "By thy long grey beard and glitt'ring eye,
> Now wherefore stop'st thou me?" '

Blank verse
Unrhymed verse written to a particular metre, generally the iambic pentameter.

C

Canto	A section of a long poem like Byron's *Don Juan*, roughly comparable to a chapter in a novel.
Cavalier Poets	A group of poets who supported King Charles I in the English Civil Wars, and who wrote witty songs and lyrics which were often about love, personal loyalty, and honour. Among them were Robert Herrick and Richard Lovelace.
Conceit	An elaborate metaphor or image, of a type frequently employed by the Metaphysical Poets. In *Witchcraft by a Picture*, for instance, John Donne imagines his portrait burning in his lover's eye or drowning in a tear.
Couplet	A pair of lines, often rhyming, such as the final lines of a Shakespearian sonnet:

'For thy sweet love remembered such wealth brings
That then I scorn to change my state with kings.'

D

Dramatic monologue	A poem narrated by an imaginary character, like Robert Browning's *My Last Duchess*.
Didactic verse	Verse intended to instruct or educate.

E

Eclogue	A short pastoral poem, based on the work of Virgil and the ancient Greeks.
Elegy	A poem written in mourning, generally for an individual.
Epic	A long narrative poem, often oral in origin, concerning heroic adventures which are usually important to the history of a nation or culture.
Epigram	A short, pointed, and usually humorous poem.
Epitaph	A short poem, designed to be inscribed on a grave or monument.
Epithalamion	A poem written in celebration of a marriage.
Epode	The third and concluding stanza of a Pindaric ode.

F

Feminine ending	An unstressed syllable at the end of a line of verse
Foot	A pattern of syllables repeated in a metrical line of verse. One of the commonest English verse forms is the pentameter, which has five feet to a line.

138

Free verse	Verse that tries to capture the natural rhythms of speech and is written without strict rhyme or metre. Noted practitioners include Walt Whitman and Ezra Pound. A similar movement in late Nineteenth Century French literature, featuring Arthur Rimbaud and Charles Baudelaire, is referred to as vers libre.

G

Georgian Poets	Early Twentieth Century group of poets including Rupert Brooke, John Masefield, Walter de la Mare, and W.H. Davies. Their poetry was often pastoral and highly idealised, and was strongly rejected by the Modernist movement. Volumes of Georgian poetry were published annually between 1912 and 1922.
Georgics	Poems about farming and the rural life, often influenced by the work of Virgil, whose *Georgics* were written under the Emperor Augustus.

H

Haiku	Japanese verse form, popularised in the west in the Twentieth Century by poets of the Modernist movement. It is a three-line poem with no rhyme, in which the first and third lines have five syllables and the second seven.
Heroic couplet	A pair of lines (couplet) which rhyme and are written in iambic pentameters, as in Alexander Pope's:

'For forms of government let fools contest
Whate'er is best administered is best.'

Horatian Ode	An ode, based on the model of the Roman poet Horace, in which all the stanzas have the same form.

I

Iambic	A form of meter in which each foot has two syllables, with the stress on the second one. The iambic pentameter, with five iambic feet to a line, is one of the most popular in English, and is the metre of Shakespeare's plays and of the vast majority of sonnets.
Image	A concrete and imaginative representation of something by comparing it or identifying it with something else. A simile, like Wordsworth's 'I wandered lonely as a cloud' is a type of

image; so is G.M. Hopkins's metaphor, when he refers to the windhover as 'kingdom of daylight's dauphin'.

Imagism Early Twentieth Century movement, influenced partly by Japanese poetry, which sought clarity and precision of expression. Imagist poems, written by such figures as Ezra Pound, D.H. Lawrence, and T.E. Hulme, tend to be short, written in free verse, and focused on a single specific image.

Internal rhyme A rhyme between two or more words within a line, rather than between the final words of two or more lines.

J

Jacobean poets Poets writing during the reign of James I (1603–1625), such as Shakespeare, John Donne, and Ben Jonson.

Juvenilia A poet's early and immature work.

K

Keatsian In the style of John Keats – often used as 'sub-Keatsian' to describe a lush, self-consciously Romantic style which fails to reach Keats's standard.

L

Lake Poets The Romantic poets Wordsworth, Coleridge, and Southey, who all lived in the Lake District and were inspired by its scenery.

Lay Originally a short poem meant to be set to music, but now used to describe any poem written in a traditional ballad style, like Macaulay's *Lays of Ancient Rome*.

Libretto Lines written to be sung as an opera or musical play.

Light verse Poetry which may or may not have a serious underlying meaning, but which is light-hearted in tone.

Limerick Form of verse popularised by the Victorian poet Edward Lear, with five lines rhyming AABBA, and with the third and fourth lines shorter than the rest.

Liverpool Poets A group of poets, most notably Roger McGough, Adrian Henri, and Roger Patten, who frequently performed together in Liverpool in the 1960s, reading humorous, often satirical, and generally anti-intellectual poetry.

Lyric Originally a poem which could be accompanied by music on the lyre, but now generally used to describe any short poem of intense personal feeling.

M

Metaphor	The imaginative identification of two acts people, or objects. While a simile would say one thing was *like* another, a metaphor would identify one thing *as* another. In *The Show*, Wilfred Owen describes the landscape at the Front, and 'its beard, that horror of harsh wire'.
Metaphysical	A term coined by Samuel Johnson to describe the poets of the early Seventeenth Century, who wrote highly intellectual verse built around complex imagery which was sustained over several lines. The term is less popular today, as it conceals important differences between individual poets.
Metre	The pattern of syllables that makes up a line of poetry. In English poetry, metre is determined by whether individual syllables are stressed or unstressed syllables, while Classical verse counts long and short syllables. A line of poetry is divided into feet, which are repeated patterns of syllables.
Middle English	The language spoken and written in England between the late Eleventh and late Fifteenth centuries. Geoffrey Chaucer, John Gower, and the Gawain Poet are among the leading writers of Middle English.
Modernism	Literary movement of the first half of the Twentieth Century led by W.B. Yeats, Ezra Pound, and T.S. Eliot, which rejected traditional forms of poetry. Imagism and free verse were two notable aspects of Modernism.

N

Neologism	The invention of new words.
Newdigate Prize	Prize awarded annually at Oxford University since the Eighteenth Century for a composition in English verse. Notable past winners include Matthew Arnold, Oscar Wilde, and Sir Andrew Motion.
Nonsense Poetry	A form of light verse which places absurd characters in absurd situations, often involving extravagant word-play, neologisms, and unexpected rhymes. Famous practitioners include Lewis Carroll and Edward Lear.

O

Occasional verse	A poem written to celebrate a specific event, such as a Royal wedding or the birth of a child.

Octave	The first eight lines of a traditional sonnet, followed by the sestet.
Ode	A lyric poem addressed to a particular person, animal, or thing, such as Keat's *Ode to a Nightingale*.
Old English	Also referred to as Anglo-Saxon; the language spoken in England from the early Fifth Century until the Norman Conquest. *Beowulf* is one of the great Old English poems.
Onomatopoeia	Words that echo the sounds they describe, such as bang or pitter-patter.

P

Pararhyme	A technique employed notably by Wilfred Owen, in which consonants but not vowels are repeated, as in escaped/scooped or moan/mourn in *Strange Meeting*.
Pastoral	Poetry dealing with rural life in a highly idealised and romanticised way.
Pentameter	A line of verse composed of five metrical feet.
Picaresque	A novel or poem, frequently comic or satirical, which tells the story of its hero's travels and adventures.
Pindaric ode	An ode, loosely modelled on the work of the Greek poet Pindar, with three distinct stanzas, known as strophe, antistrophe, and epode
Poet Laureate	In Britain, the poet appointed, originally by the monarch but now by the Prime Minister, to write in celebration of national occasions. John Dryden was the first official holder of the post, but several earlier poets, including Skelton, Spenser and Jonson, are considered to have been unofficial Poets Laureate. The appointment was originally for life, but is now made for a period of 10 years. The US Senate established a similar post in 1985.
Pre-Raphaelite Brotherhood	A Nineteenth Century group of poets, including Dante Gabriel Rossetti and William Morris, who found inspiration in mediaeval (i.e. before the Renaissance and the era of Raphael) art and literature.
Professor of Poetry	An appointment at Oxford University, given since 1708 to a leading poet selected by the University's Convocation. It lasts for five years, and the recipient is expected to deliver three lectures a year on subjects of his or her own choosing.
Prosody	The study of the mechanical structure of verse, including rhyme, metre, and stanzas.

Glossary

Prothalamion	A poem written before a wedding to celebrate the event.
Pulitzer Prize	One of a number of prizes awarded each year in the US since 1917 for achievement in the fields of journalism, literature, and musical composition.

Q

Quatrain	A four-line stanza.

R

Rhyme	The effect of repeated similar vowel sounds, usually at the end of lines of verse. Rhymes occurring in a single line are referred to as 'internal rhyme'. Rhyme schemes are recorded as ABAB or AABBCC, etc, when each letter represents a different rhyme.
Rhymers' Club	A group of poets, founded in 1890, which used to meet at the Cheshire Cheese pub in Fleet Street, London, to read and discuss poetry. Members included W.B. Yeats, Lionel Johnson, and Richard Le Gallienne.
Romantic	Term often used to describe the work of poets such as Wordsworth, Keats, Shelley and Byron. Romantic poets valued self-expression and the passionate expression of the individual over the balance, order and intellectualism of the poets of the Eighteenth Century.

S

Satire	A poem which ridicules perceived vices such as hypocrisy, greed, or vulgarity.
Scansion	The study of the structure of a line of poetry to establish its metrical pattern.
Scottish Literary Renaissance	Twentieth Century Scottish literary movement encouraging the use of the Scots dialect of Robert Burns. It was led by Hugh MacDiarmid.
Sestet	The final six lines of a traditional sonnet, preceded by the octet.
Simile	A comparison made in order to create a vivid description. A simile may be short, as in Andrew Marvell's 'the youthful hue Sits on thy skin like morning dew', or it may be developed over many lines. Homer's *Iliad* and *Odyssey* are particularly known for these 'extended similes'.

Skeltonic	A form of verse devised by John Skelton in the late Fifteenth Century. Its characteristics include short, irregular lines with repeated rhymes.
Sonnet	A short poem of 14 lines, usually in iambic pentameters, and often with a division between the first eight lines (octave) and the last six (sestet). Different variations include Petrarchan, Shakespearean, and Miltonic sonnets.
Stanza	A number of lines which, grouped together, make up a unit of a poem, separated from the next stanza by a blank line. A two-line stanza is known as a couplet, three lines as a tercet, and four lines as a quatrain.
Strophe	The first stanza of a Pindaric ode.

7

Tanka	Non-rhyming Japanese verse form of seven lines, popularised in the west in the Twentieth Century by the Modernist movement. It has exactly 31 syllables – five lines in the first and third lines, and seven in the second, fourth and fifth.
Tercet	A three line stanza.
Thirties Poets	A group of 1930s writers largely dominated by W.H. Auden, and including Louis MacNeice, Cecil Day-Lewis, and Stephen Spender. However, the term is less popular today, since it disguises important differences between the various poets.
Triolet	Eight line stanza form with only two rhymes, in which the first two lines are repeated as the last two lines, and the first line is repeated as the fourth. Frances Cornford's *To a Fat Lady Seen from a Train* is a famous example.
Typography	The design and arrangement of type on a page.

V

Vers libre	See Free verse.
Villanelle	A complex 19-line poem of five triplets with a final quatrain. The ABA rhyme scheme is repeated throughout; the first line is repeated as the sixth, twelfth and eighteenth, and the third line as the ninth, fifteenth, and nineteenth. It is based on the verses and choruses of a traditional French song form.

Index